Border Boating

Border Boating

Twelve Cruises through the San Juan and Gulf Islands
by
Phyllis and Bill Bultmann

Pacific Search Press

Pacific Search Press, 715 Harrison Street, Seattle, Washington 98109
© 1979 by Pacific Search Press. All rights reserved
Printed in the United States of America

Designed by Paula Schlosser
Photography by Phyllis and Bill Bultmann
Maps by Judy Petry
Illustration of Galiano (or Malaspina) Galleries is courtesy
    of Provincial Archives, Victoria, British Columbia

Cover: Sidney Customs Wharf

Library of Congress Cataloging in Publication Data

Bultmann, Phyllis.
    Border boating.

    Bibliography: p.
    1. Boats and boating—Washington (State)—San Juan
Islands—Guide-books. 2. Boats and boating—British
Columbia—Gulf Islands—Guide-books. 3. San Juan
Islands—Description and travel—Guide-books. 4. Gulf
Islands—Description and travel—Guide-books. I. Bultmann,
Bill, joint author. II. Title.
GV776.W22S262   917   78-23280
ISBN 0-914718-37-1

Acknowledgments

We are indebted to many people—too many to name in a brief space—for help in the research that produced this book. However, we particularly want to thank the following people for their ready, cheerful answers to our many questions: Bob Little, District Supervisor of the Washington State Parks and Recreation Commission; Bill Lausch, Superintendent of Harbors, Port of Bellingham; Pete Granger, Field Agent for Washington Sea Grant; Frank Richards, editor of the *Gulf Islands Driftwood*; and the rangers of the San Juan Island National Historical Park.

We also want to express our appreciation to the editors of *Sea* magazine, who encouraged us to write boating stories about our experiences in the islands. Much of the information that appears in this book was first gathered for feature stories in *Sea*. Many thanks to Chris Caswell, Harry Monahan, and Elyse Mintey.

Contents

Water and Sun and Pebbled Shore

Most of the landfalls between Canada's Vancouver Island and the North American mainland are hilltops clothed in conifers and outlined with rocks. Variety is supplied by an occasional sun-baked sandspit, a naked igneous mound, or an enclosed lagoon like Fisherman Bay on Lopez Island.

On Sidney Island in British Columbia, Sidney Spit darts northwestward almost a mile, a zigzag of lightning. It is golden with sea grasses. Beached logs lie along its crest like tossed jackstraws. From the sand you can see the snowy crests of the Olympics defining the southern horizon. From a headland overlooking the spit's beaches you can—on a clear day—see Mount Baker, an hour's drive inland from the Washington coast.

Much nearer, dotting the surface of the Northwest's great inland sea, the islands rise in overlapping ranks, indifferent to the international boundary line that men have drawn on the waters. You see Gooch Island (Canada) against Stuart Island (United States) against South Pender and Saturna (both in Canada). Southeastward, the bare back of Mandarte Island (Canada) rises like a monstrous hippo in the foreground, and beyond it to the east are Spieden Island and a tall, pale shape that is Orcas (both in the United States).

The nearness of these landfalls to each other produces the phenomenon that we call "border boating." If you are on Sidney, Spieden calls to you; from Orcas, Saturna is tempting; from Bedwell Harbour it is only an hour by powerboat to Roche Harbor; from Sucia, the imposing bulk of Salt Spring Island beckons. With so many temptations for the eye and the imagination, it is no wonder that

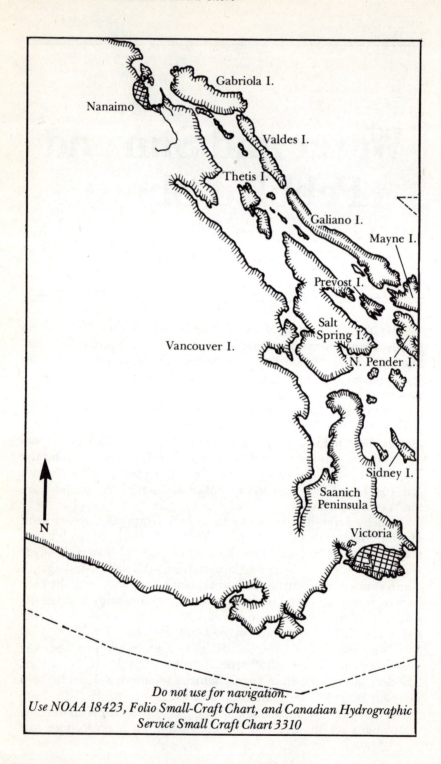

Nanaimo

Gabriola I.

Valdes I.

Thetis I.

Galiano I.

Mayne I.

Prevost I.

Salt Spring I.

Vancouver I.

N. Pender I.

Sidney I.

Saanich Peninsula

N

Victoria

Do not use for navigation.
Use NOAA 18423, Folio Small-Craft Chart, and Canadian Hydrographic
Service Small Craft Chart 3310

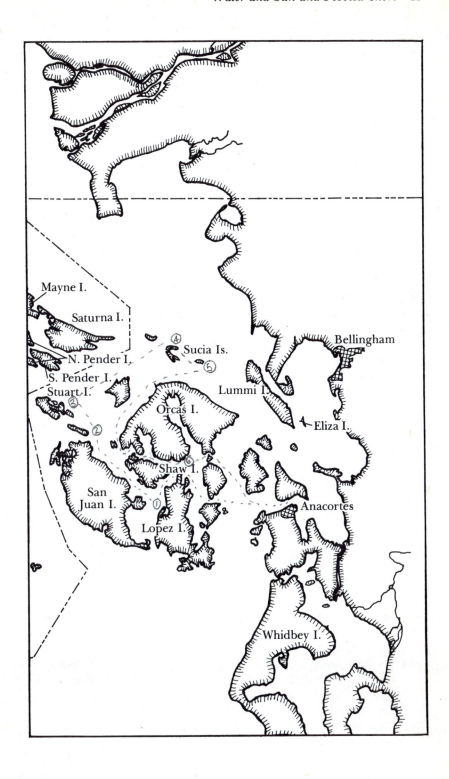

those who can reach the border islands cross back and forth, to enjoy them all.

What exactly is the peculiar magic of these wooded islands and rocky shores? What makes Northwest boatmen head for the San Juans, push on to the Gulf Islands, then swear to return again and again—as often as possible?

The islands are elusive, uncrowded, almost uncounted. Perhaps that explains their appeal. Some sources claim there are over 170 islands—others count up to 500—in the San Juan archipelago alone. Official surveys disagree. Whatever the number, you cannot see all of them in one cruise. You cannot really see all the San Juan and Gulf islands in ten years, as we know from trying. Together these islands create hundreds of miles of protected channels, coves, inlets, and harbors that welcome small craft. They stand up from the sea in a thousand irregular shapes. They form a yachtsman's paradise. Even forty years is not enough time to dull the appetite of an island-happy skipper, once he has tasted the fare. Old-timers by the score will testify to their annually renewed excitement, their hunger for "another look at Orcas" or Pender or Shaw.

In this book are a dozen plans for border boating. They are only a beginning. You can expand on them at will, lengthening, shortening, doubling back. You will see that while the twelve cruises are described separately, some can be combined to make longer trips. Cruise One by itself will take no more than three days. If, however, you want a longer excursion, Cruises One and Two, linked at the junction point of Turn Island, will last four to seven days, depending on your boat. Cruises One, Two, and Three, taken together, add up to a ten-day venture, and if you combine the first four plans you may well be out on the water for a fortnight. When calculating your total traveling time, do not forget to add the amount of time it will take you to reach each departure point and to return eventually to your home port.

No two skippers will use the same amount of time for these excursions, of course. Since a cruise is not a race, it calls for little speed and anticipates many slow hours spent ashore—exploring, beach-combing, fishing, picnicking, sampling coffee shops—or merely loafing in the cockpit of a moored vessel. A sailboat may also have to spend long hours waiting for wind, so we estimate time needed to travel under both power and sail, and we mention extra overnight stops in case you need them. Most of our experience in these waters has been aboard small, planing-hull cruisers. Our *Sea Scribbler* is a twenty-seven-foot Bayliner. But our powerboat estimates make ample allowance for slower, displacement-hull vessels, and our sailing estimates are based on a running speed of four knots.

The first four cruises concentrate on the San Juan Islands, although Cruise Three takes you briefly across the border for a visit to one of the world's most beautiful gardens.

Cruises Five through Eight emphasize the pleasures of border boating between the northern San Juans and the nearer Gulf Islands. As with the first grouping, they can be undertaken separately or linked together for longer cruises.

Cruise Nine and Cruise Ten are long runs requiring two weeks or more apiece and duplicating fragments of our shorter cruises. In general, they anticipate more hours in motion, longer unbroken stretches of cruising, and the coverage of much more territory than the plans in the first eight cruises. Cruise Nine, for example, departs from Shilshole Bay Marina in Seattle and has for its outbound destination Nanaimo, in British Columbia. Cruise Ten, departing from Bellingham, runs north to Ganges, then south to Victoria, returning through Middle Channel to Bellingham.

Cruise Eleven concentrates on small marine parks on both sides of the border. With rare exceptions, the parks visited on this cruise will be those that other cruises miss.

Cruise Twelve follows the routes of the Spanish explorers. The latter, after months on the open ocean and lifetimes spent at sea, did not hesitate—even in a gale—to cross the Strait of Juan de Fuca and similar obstreperous channels whenever they pleased. You should feel free merely to sample their itinerary. Adhere to the stretches of it that suit your own comfort and convenience, remembering that small-craft warnings fly often on Juan de Fuca. Explorer Francisco Eliza did not command a thirty-foot cabin cruiser, and you yourself have no obligation to produce a nautical chart of hitherto unknown waters.

Amenities useful to boatmen are mentioned here and there throughout the cruise chapters. In addition, the sections at the end of the book group them together in lists. We ask you to use these lists with caution. The life of a business enterprise in the islands is precarious: marinas go under, laundromats break down, groceries fold, restaurants lose their chefs. When planning to stop for essential supplies, such as fuel or food, you should phone ahead to make sure the establishment you have in mind is functioning and will be open for business at the hour you arrive. Also, where it is possible to reserve moorage in advance, you would be wise to phone in your name and estimated time of arrival. Summer weekends are crowded, and most unreserved moorage is taken by 1300 or 1400 hours. If you do not like to anchor, tie up early!

In general, the cruises assume that you can sleep on your boat. However, campsites and shore accommodations—where they exist—are identified to help those who cannot. Distress frequencies on CB and VHF radios and the stations that monitor them are listed in "Safety Reminders."

Here are the twelve cruises. May you enjoy them as much as we have—over and over again—during the past ten years!

The San Juans and Saanich

The San Juan Islands—the principal focus of Cruises One, Two, and Four—are agreeably near the dense populations of upper Puget Sound. A kind of axis exists, linking Seattle to Friday Harbor on San Juan. A large percentage of Northwestern boatmen confine their cruising to this axis and the round clump of islands at its end.

Friday Harbor, located inside the islands as if facing the hole in a doughnut, is the seat of San Juan County. Not all the islands commonly called "the San Juans" fall within this one governmental unit, however. For our purposes, we use the larger or extended meaning of that phrase, because good cruising is to be found among the fringe islands that technically belong to Skagit and Whatcom counties, and crossing Rosario Strait to reach them is likely to be the high point of a day's run. Cypress and Sinclair, Lummi and Guemes islands all figure in these first cruises because to cruising yachtsmen the waterways are the thoroughfares of travel. The landforms to port and starboard, fore and aft, frame our prospect. You may head for Orcas, but Sinclair will lie on the water astern. And while coasting along the southwestern face of Spieden Island in San Juan County, you will have Saanich Peninsula with its fringe of small islands on your port quarter.

So we have looped Cruise Three across Haro Strait to enable you to visit Butchart Gardens, the incredible flower-filled quarry on Vancouver Island. And we have looped Cruise Four out of San Juan County to encircle Lummi Island.

You will notice that the names of the San Juans are primarily Spanish in origin, reflecting their discovery by Spanish explorers in the eighteenth century. But Hawaiian, Indian, English, and American names appear here and there, and always for a reason. Friday Harbor, for instance, was named for Kanaka Joe Friday, an early settler of Hawaiian ancestry. Kanaka Bay on the outer rim of San Juan Island was also named for Hawaiian settlers. Ships' names and the names of ships' officers—English, Spanish, and American—appear on mountains and hills, bays and channels. Lummi Island derives its name from the Lummi Indian tribe, which originally enjoyed its sheltered coves, and Cypress' name was simply a mistake. The trees that gave this island its name are in fact cedars.

The people who live (and have lived) on these islands are individualists. They do not accept any change without the expression of diverse and often contentious opinions. Their houses are not built according to any one accepted architectural pattern; they have been known to raise foxes rather than sheep, market venison rather than beef. They are free spirits. Cruising in their midst, you may well feel your spirit loosening up a bit, too.

Before beginning Cruise One, we think we should issue at least a mild warning to new boatmen and to boatmen who have done all their previous boating in other parts of the country. Skippers should expect certain special characteristics of wind and water. Winds are fluky, both as to direction and force. In the summer, some days are completely calm, others feature occasional thirty-knot gusts. Tidal currents are strong in most narrow channels; tide tables should be aboard so that you can determine the times of slack water. Tide rips are encountered occasionally but should cause you little trouble beyond a bumpy few minutes. Often they can be avoided by referring to charts or by noting rippled areas in the water ahead of you. Seaweed masses, the largest of which are indicated on charts, are found in many shallow coves and bights. Drifting logs constitute the most familiar hazard, and every prudent skipper keeps a constant watch to avoid contact with telephone-pole-sized drifters. If in a powerboat, he instantly throttles back and alters course sharply when a crew member sings out, "Deadhead dead ahead!"

That caveat clearly stated, it is time now to board your vessel and take off.

Cruise
One

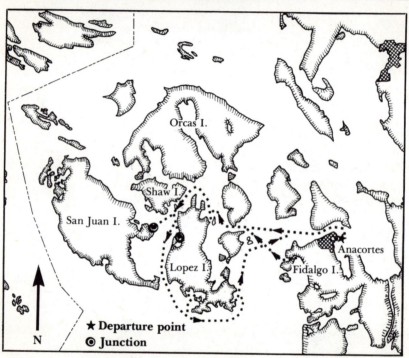

Do not use for navigation.
Use NOAA 18423, Folio Small-Craft Chart

Loop around Lopez

Point of departure: Anacortes, Washington

Course: via Guemes Channel or Burrows Bay, Rosario Strait, Thatcher Pass, East Sound, Upright Channel, Middle Channel, Strait of Juan de Fuca; return up Rosario Strait to Anacortes

Stops: Spencer Spit, Fisherman Bay and/or Turn Island, Watmough Bay, Hunter Bay

Length of cruise: approximately 46 nautical miles to Anacortes; 18 nautical miles to junction with Cruise Two

Duration on power: 2 days

Duration on sail: 2 to 3 days

Overnight moorage:

First night: Fisherman Bay or Turn Island

Second night: Watmough Bay or Hunter Bay

Junction point for Cruise Two: Fisherman Bay or Turn Island State Marine Park

Two Tranquil Days

It is an early weekend in May. The day is warm, the breeze light, and Mount Baker—looming grandly to the north—wears a thick mantle of new snow. What a perfect time for an overnight shakedown cruise that will give you a jump on the summer!

You are poised in Anacortes, ready to go. Your boat is tied to a visitor's wharf, or it is dangling in a lift, about to be launched. Where exactly are you?

Anacortes is a small city about sixty miles north of Seattle on Fidalgo Island, a landmass that feels and looks like mainland. At first hearing, the name Anacortes has a Spanish ring to it, but in fact it was bestowed by the city's founder in honor of his wife—Anna Curtis. The thin thread of navigable water that qualifies Fidalgo as an island is long and curving, like a river. Called the Swinomish Channel, it is much loved by the skippers of Seattle-based small craft that are too large to be trailered. By easing through the somewhat intricate bends of the Swinomish, they can reach the San Juans without having to brave the formidable Strait of Juan de Fuca.

Crossing the Swinomish at irregular intervals are four bridges that carry six lanes of traffic and a railroad track. Hence Fidalgo Island appears to be sewn to the mainland with threads of steel and macadam. Each summer, boat trailers roll across those threads by the hundreds to park in the Port of Anacortes or in the trailer lots at Flounder Bay, on the western edge of the town.

Where it fronts on Guemes Channel, Fidalgo Island presents a broad, flattened coastline. Projections like hammerheads enlarge its northeastern and northwestern corners. The city of Anacortes covers much of this broad coastline, with its business district concentrated on the northeastern tip. Two spots are especially important to skippers who want to explore the San Juan Islands: Cap Sante Boat Haven, the port-maintained public marina in downtown Anacortes, and the less frequented, privately owned Skyline Marina in Flounder Bay, where temporary accommodations for small craft are also available. Seattle boatmen arriving up the outside or western shore of Whidbey and Fidalgo islands tend increasingly to put in at the floats of Skyline.

Because most Northwest skippers reach our Anacortes departure point by trailering or piloting their boats from other places—either in or out of the state of Washington—we shall assume an overnight stay, or a launch, at one of these two shelters. That way you will be ready to go on Saturday morning.

The first destination on Cruise One is Spencer Spit State Park; you will find much to savor and absorb as you head for it. Emerging from Cap Sante Boat Haven through the Capsante Waterway, you hook to port and run westward down Guemes Channel. If leaving from Skyline Marina, you cross a bit of Burrows Bay, then cruise between the high mounds of Burrows Island and Fidalgo Head. Each of these passages is beautiful and sheltered, but the latter may well have tidal currents strong enough to argue against a start at flood or ebb tide. Cross when the tide is standing· and you should have no trouble.

As you begin the transit of Rosario Strait, you will head slightly north of a small, very noticeable landfall on the opposite side of this great waterway. The landfall is James Island, which lies due west of Shannon Point. When you come abeam of James, you will have entered San Juan County and the San Juan Islands.

It will take half an hour or more to cross Rosario Strait, depending on the weather and your boat's form of propulsion. There is time to look around. Abeam to the south is the widening mouth of Rosario Strait where it opens into the Strait of Juan de Fuca. Up this avenue came the exploring schooners—Spanish, English, and American— two centuries ago.

So much frustration was experienced in the dozen or so years that followed 1790! Tall masted, moving cautiously under light sail, vessel after vessel came seeking the fabled Northwest Passage that would connect the Pacific with the Atlantic at a convenient latitude for shipping. The explorers nosed up narrow channels, took frequent soundings (with lead lines, of course; no fathometer in those days), and still managed to run aground from time to time in the shallow waters from Padilla Bay north. As you look astern, and abeam to starboard, you can see some of the routes they took. The *Mexicana* and the *Sutil* explored Guemes Channel in June of 1792, two days after Peter Puget and Joseph Whidbey anchored and camped ashore on the westernmost promontory of Whidbey Island. Lummi Indians in canoes loaded with wild strawberries watched them, no doubt wondering where all the traffic was coming from.

Your view to the north changes rapidly, opening new vistas as you reach farther and farther across Rosario Strait. Cypress Island, a mountainous, much indented landmass that even today is host to little habitation, parts the waters that stream toward the international border on each incoming tide. On the southern coast of Cypress are a number of enormous erratic boulders unrelated to the native rocks, moved here from somewhere farther north by the glaciers that covered this region in the Ice Age. Bellingham Channel, a slender but deep passage, divides Cypress from Guemes Island. This tempting waterway leads your eye toward the high, knife-sharp ridge of Lummi Island, one of the most distinctive shapes in the San Juans. Today large freighters and heavily burdened tugs ply this channel, taking the place of freighting schooners under sail, but the most frequently seen vessels are small craft, like yours.

By now you are almost across the shining expanse of Rosario Strait. Looking astern you see the long "yellow bluff" of Guemes Island, an unusually beautiful landmark that is also famous as the headquarters of a late-nineteenth-century smuggler named Kelly. And northward you can see around Cypress Island to the narrower reaches of Rosario Strait where, eventually, the heaviest northbound traffic is fed into Canada's Strait of Georgia. Far in the distance is the tall, pale blue line of the Canadian Coast Range, usually frosted along its entire length with generous layers of snow. The long, low ribbon of land in the foreground is the inhabited portion of Lummi Island.

The great exploring and trading vessels are a memory now; the Indian war canoes are brought out only to race visiting tribes on occasions such as the Lummis' stommish, an annual tribal festival. Nevertheless, you may be sharing the waters with much exciting traffic. Ponderous Washington State ferries run through Thatcher Pass ahead of you, serving the larger, inhabited San Juan islands (Orcas, San Juan, Shaw, and Lopez). Occasionally on the Vessel Traffic System (VTS)—the controlled lanes of Rosario Strait—you will see freighters, or tugs pulling barges of sawdust to paper mills, or commercial fishing boats. Sometimes a navy vessel or the Coast Guard's *Point Richmond* will go by.

Now you have James Island on the port quarter. Shaped like a dumbbell or a dog's bone, it is one of the smallest of the San Juans to be encountered in these cruises. Fortunately for us boating enthusiasts, it has been made into a state marine park, accessible only by water craft. On this fine weekend, it looks enormously attractive in its sparkling green cover of fir and cedar but, unless Cruise One is to take a week or more, you will not stop today to explore its attractions. (When you are ready for Cruise Eleven, a tour of marine parks, you will stay overnight at James Island and explore it fully.)

North of James, between Decatur and Blakely islands, is Thatcher Pass, an opening in the wall of the San Juans, and you set your course for it. Look north once more, just before you enter the pass; this is your best view of sharp-pointed Eagle Cliff on Cypress

Island, a landmark that rises against the ever-present backdrop of Lummi Island.

You leave Rosario Strait's more exposed waters, and if the wind has gotten up, you do so thankfully. It takes only a few minutes to reach the inner San Juan passages through Thatcher's broad doorway. As your bow swings around into East Sound, you see a number of small islands, some as symmetrical as scoops of ice cream. The largest of these, Frost Island, is thinly forested, but its bulk hides Spencer Spit until you are well to the north of the island.

Rosario Strait is frequently rough and stormy, but what about East Sound, running long and slim into the heart of Orcas Island? The odds for a smooth passage are in your favor here, especially between May and October. It is likely that you will approach Lopez Island over a gentle ripple, and the distant stretch of East Sound that opens to the north will gleam harmlessly in the sun. The water can occasionally be rough, of course. We have hit such a heavy chop in East Sound that our small cruiser bounced like a cork. In any case, ten minutes or so will bring you up on a mooring buoy off the north shore of Spencer Spit State Park on Lopez Island.

Spencer Spit is not exclusively a marine park. It can be reached by car from a large and populous island that is served by an automobile-bearing ferry. As a result, many land-traveling campers compete with boatmen for campsites. A campsite charge is levied by park officials, who allot the areas on a first-come, first-served basis.

On this cruise, however, you are stopping only for lunch. It is early in the day, and you should find several of the mooring buoys free to tie to, without any charge.

Spencer Spit is one of the handsomest of the parks in the San Juans. A long, low tongue of sand crested by piled and twisted logs, the spit projects outward from the northeastern shoulder of Lopez Island. It shelters flocks of ducks, Canada geese, and shorebirds such as turnstones, sandpipers, and dunlins. It invites picnicking, clam digging, beachcombing, and even swimming in the warmest months. You can afford two or three hours ashore—wading, hiking, building sand castles, collecting driftwood treasures—because the run around Lopez to Fisherman Bay for the night's moorage is not long. Spencer Spit is a wonderful treat for the younger members of the family who wish to stretch their legs after a morning's boat ride.

Where only a short while ago you had to anchor off Spencer Spit if you came by boat, the Washington State Parks and Recreation Commission has now installed eleven mooring buoys—eight north of the tongue, three south. You go ashore by dinghy unless the design of your boat allows you to beach it. The park has water from a well, and pit toilets, with more modern restroom facilities planned for the near future. Picnic tables and trash receptacles are maintained, all of them back among the trees at the base of the spit where they do not detract from the spare, almost oriental aspect of the park.

Near the end of the spit, not far from Frost Island, there is a small, rough-hewn cabin, once a dwelling, which shows the effects of countless winter winds and rains. Cracks gape between its beams now, and the roof fits only here and there. The earth and sand of its floor dribble out in small sand slides beneath its walls, and fires have blackened some of its timbers. No doubt there are those who want to pull it down—let us hope they have not yet succeeded. You can look at it (or out from it, toward the much-broken southern profile of Lopez) and think satisfying thoughts about the early settlers.

If you are a good walker, there is a road that leads from the park up into the island's farm acreage. Every bend brings majestic views of bays and headlands, distant islands and rolling fields. There are herds of sheep on Lopez, and orchards, and wild berries (not ripe in spring-time, but you may elect to try this cruise later in the year). Photographers among you will find old houses, rills, rocks, and gnarled trees to engage your skill. Birds are numerous and fearless in the farmlands. Woodpeckers hammer ancient fence posts perhaps no more than twenty-five feet away from you. Great blue herons pose artfully along the shoreline. And belted kingfishers plummet into the water from overhanging branches.

Not long ago, you may remember, a good way to get a laugh was to call someone a bird watcher. Today (thanks to whom—the Sierra Club? the Audubon Society? the threat of oil spills?), a birder poised behind a telescope-bearing tripod soon collects a curious and respectful audience. If you are a bird enthusiast, set up your gear on Spencer Spit. You can scan the trees on Frost Island for hawks and eagles, the shallow waters to the south for ducks and loons. In the spring you might see a king eider or—to your surprise—a porpoise or a whale.

But lunch is over and it is time to push on. As you loop north around Humphrey Head, you can see the gap of Peavine Pass off the starboard quarter, and beyond is a backdrop of Lummi Island. When abeam of Upright Head on Lopez Island you swing south into Upright Channel. This passage is a high point of the cruise, not only because the views are splendid, but because the hazards are a challenge. Somehow the ferry routes all seem to converge at Upright Head—ferries to Orcas; ferries to Sidney, British Columbia; ferries to Friday Harbor. Sometimes it is almost too much for small craft. Everyone in our family remembers the time, early in our boating years, when we were approaching this spot in our small cabin cruiser. Phyl, a conscientious and very green first mate, was learning to pilot. Nearing Upright Head, nervously but irrevocably in charge of the helm, she was suddenly beset by ferries. One was closing on the starboard beam from Harney Channel; another loomed bow-on between Shaw Island and Lopez Island; a third looked set to attack near Humphrey Head.

She spun the wheel 180 degrees, like a hydrofoil driver going around the mark.

"Hey! What're you doing?" exclaimed Bill, holding on.

"Getting out of here!" she cried, making for Obstruction Pass at full throttle.

The threatening ferries, proceeding on their appointed routes, actually were far away. But a ferry is so big it can look awfully close when it is not. We have never gone down Upright Channel without sharing it, either ahead or astern, with one of these white and green moving mountains. They are beautiful, and not really dangerous at all—so long as you stay out of their way.

But there are other hazards. Deadheads and driftwood of all sizes seem to accumulate in Upright Channel, so the wise skipper will post a "deadhead" watch in this area.

Upright Channel is constricted at one spot by a sandspit that is justly famous. This projection, called Flat Point, is shorter than Spencer Spit and capable of supporting denser vegetation as well. A line of conifers, oddly shaped and pruned by the winds that sweep up the open waters to the south, reaches out almost to the end of Flat Point. From any direction they form an entrancing picture on the most photographed and painted promontory in the islands.

As you near the meeting of the waters where San Juan Channel and Upright Channel flow together, you will be looking for Fisherman Bay, your stop for the night. At first you will not see it, because the mouth of Fisherman Bay is well hidden. All you see at a glance is a wooded and unbroken shoreline. But look again. A set of channel markers leads toward an inward-curving sandspit. The channel looks remarkably narrow.

At this point the uninitiated skipper may hesitate, but he need not. Ahead lies a reverse letter-S channel, well marked and capable of floating at zero tide any vessel that draws no more than five and one-half feet. The channel is perhaps three hundred yards long, and beautiful. Stay close to the markers and you will have no problems. We have seen small sailboats run the channel under sail, but we advise sailors to use the auxiliary motor instead, unless they are old-timers to Lopez, because winds and currents here can be freaky. Negotiating this twisting approach to the bay is one of the delights of this cruise.

Once inside Fisherman Bay, you may anchor in a protected corner or rent space at the Islander Lopez Resort's floats. If you choose to anchor, check your tide tables carefully. The south end of

Municipal building in Lopez Village

the bay goes dry on a minus tide. For your evening meal, you may prepare dinner in your galley, picnic at a fire ring ashore, dine at the Islander Lopez, or stroll up the road to the Galley Restaurant. Whatever your choice, you will watch the sun drop beyond the bay, making its surface opalescent and throwing into black silhouette the promontory that shelters this sheet of hidden water.

Our own practice is to tie up at the Islander Lopez. When you pay the float rental fee here, your party has access to a Jacuzzi pool and, in summer, a heated swimming pool, and is only a few steps from the dining facilities and the weekend entertainment in the bar.

If you are among the fortunate few who have room in their vessels for bicycles, bring them. Lopez is ideal cycling ground. The roads rise and fall over gently mounded hills. Cars and trucks are infrequent, and a twenty-mile ride takes you through much serene, smiling countryside. Old split-rail fences—unpainted surfaces shining silver in the sun—zigzag along the roadway, outlining many of the early Lopez farmsteads.

If you do not bring bicycles, stroll. From Fisherman Bay, an easy walk of under two miles brings you to Lopez Village. Approaching from above, you will see fine old buildings that evoke island life of a hundred years ago. A new market in the midst of the old town buildings is a convenience, and on the flats between the village and the bay, you may see a set of beached reefnetters with a line of gulls perched on their tilted fish-viewing platforms.

Golfers will find an island taxi service ready to transport them from the Islander Lopez to the public links of Lopez Island. Divers can rent equipment for submerged shoreline explorations, and fishing is good near Fisherman Bay, as its name suggests.

In spite of these attractions, you may decide to turn your backs on Lopez and spend the night at Turn Island State Marine Park instead. The park is located directly across San Juan Channel from the hidden entrance to Fisherman Bay. Nestled close to San Juan Island, Turn Island is small—thirty-five acres in all—but large enough to have a beautiful sandy beach and a magnificent nature trail cut through the woods along its entire shoreline. Fire rings, picnic tables, four campsites, and pit toilets are available. It is a wildlife preserve where you can see deer, a variety of waterfowl, and an occasional land bird. Tidewater creatures abound on its rock-strewn shores, and wild flowers bloom on its headlands.

On the side of the island protected by the nearby bulk of San Juan are three mooring buoys. Try to arrive early so you can tie up to one of these. Strong tidal currents close to shore make anchoring difficult. At night, the water will probably rock your boat rather vigorously, because there is always a heavy flow of marine traffic through San Juan Channel. To us, the pleasures of the park are worth it; besides, a little rocking lulls one to sleep.

On your second day, you must make a decision about your course. If the weather is good, you will want to proceed around the southern tip of Lopez Island, which is a rocky, jagged, starkly beautiful shore that forms the eastern edge of Middle Channel and part of the northern rim of the Strait of Juan de Fuca. But this course takes you for some five miles through the strait itself. If our Northwest weather has turned stormy, you will be uncomfortable on Juan de Fuca, and in that case you can retrace your course for home, protecting your vessel and crew from the strait's buffeting.

If you have time for a longer excursion, now is the moment to start up San Juan Channel on Cruise Two.

However, let us assume you are going on around Lopez this time. There are many enchanting coves and bays to explore after you have turned away from the sleek lighthouse across the channel on the tip of San Juan Island. The skipper of a power cruiser, knowing he can make it back to Anacortes in under an hour as soon as he has rounded Watmough Head, can take time to poke into all of them: Davis Bay, Mackaye Harbor, Barlow Bay, Outer Bay. Beyond Iceberg Point he can enjoy the deep, protected inlets of Aleck Bay, Hughes Bay, and McArdle Bay. On a calm, windless day, he might wish to drop a hook in Outer Bay for a short time and let his crew dinghy ashore to search for agates at Agate Beach Park.

All of these indentations are strewn with rocks and barely submerged reefs, so careful attention to the nautical chart is essential, not only while running close in but even out around the points and headlands. Be particularly careful to avoid the crescent of water south of Long Island and Charles Island, where rocks abound. Tiny Hall Island is right in the middle of this reef, and while it is visible enough, the others are not. Approach Mackaye Harbor from slightly west of

Reef-netters beached at Fisherman Bay on Lopez Island

McArdle Bay on Lopez Island

south, not too far from Iceberg Point.

From Watmough Head, the southeastern tip of Lopez, your course lies north to the White Cliff on Decatur and then across Rosario Strait to Anacortes once again.

You may want to extend this cruise another night but without undertaking the considerably longer distances that Cruise Two involves. If so, try exploring the eastern face of Lopez Island. You can anchor comfortably for the second night in Watmough Bay, entering it north of Boulder Island. It is shallow but the bottom is good for anchoring, and you are close to Lopez Pass, which admits you to Lopez Sound. Keep an eye on the tides if you use this anchorage.

You may prefer to enter the sound and make for Hunter Bay, where you are bound to find other cruising boats at anchor on any pleasant weekend. Inside Lopez Sound you can do a lot of beautiful, low-key cruising. There is even a small wharf at the little town of Decatur on Decatur Island. Much of the water in the sound is protected from winds so that boats may be anchored against almost any shore, and the mud flats to the south (in Mud Bay) shelter much interesting birdlife. Fingerlings swim in the shallows.

When you are ready for home, you can emerge through Thatcher Pass, cross Rosario Strait, and approach Anacortes in time, if the weather favors you, to watch Mount Baker glow pink with the setting sun.

Cruise
Two

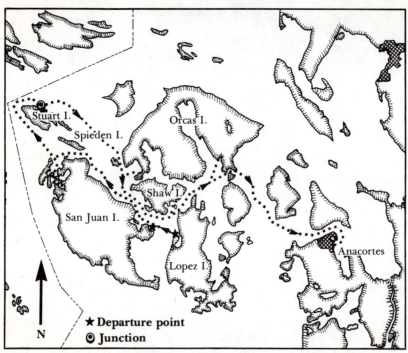

Stuart I.

Spieden I.

Orcas I.

Shaw I.

San Juan I.

Lopez I.

Anacortes

★ **Departure point**
◉ **Junction**

N

Do not use for navigation.
Use NOAA 18423, Folio Small-Craft Chart

Turn Island to Turn Point, and Return

Point of departure: Fisherman Bay on Lopez Island or Turn Island State Marine Park

Course: via San Juan Channel and Spieden Channel to Turn Point, Stuart Island; through Haro Strait, Spring Passage, Wasp Islands, San Juan Channel, Upright Channel, East Sound, Obstruction Pass; return down Rosario Strait to Anacortes

Stops: Friday Harbor, Roche Harbor, Garrison Bay, Reid Harbor and/or Prevost Harbor, Jones Island, Indian Cove on Shaw Island, Olga on Orcas Island

Length of cruise: approximately 40 nautical miles out and back to Turn Island; 26 nautical miles to junction with Cruise Three

Duration on power: 3 days

Duration on sail: 3 to 6 days

Overnight moorage:
First night: Roche Harbor or Garrison Bay
Second night: Prevost Harbor

Junction point for Cruise Three: Prevost Harbor

Cruising through History

Cruise Two begins either at Turn Island State Marine Park, just off the east side of San Juan Island, or at Fisherman Bay on the west side of Lopez Island. (See Cruise One for a description of facilities at these two moorages.)

As you enter San Juan Channel from Fisherman Bay or from Turn Island—with the long bulk of San Juan Island spreading to the west—you may find yourself thinking of the past. Images of Spanish ships and explorers come to mind, or men wearing eighteenth-century plumed hats or the uniforms of Civil War days.

Perhaps you will think back to the summer of 1859 when San Juan Island affected the diplomacy of two major powers—one pre-eminent in the world, the other just emerging—and almost provoked a war between them.

If you like to mull over events of the past while looking at the ground (or water) on which they took place, slow your boat north of Turn Island and look south toward Middle Channel, the narrow opening between Lopez and San Juan islands.

On a fair, clear afternoon in the spring of 1792, the *Chatham*, smaller of the two vessels in the expedition of Captain George Vancouver, nosed through that opening. She was a warship, an armed tender. The first European-style vessel to enter the San Juan archipelago's inner passages, she carried ten deck cannon and a crew of twenty-five seamen.

Dugout canoes, paddled by Indians of many Northwest tribes, had plied these waters for centuries before any European ships did. Beached in countless small coves, hauled out for spring encampments, for clam feasts, deer hunts, and berry-picking expeditions, they had probed every bight and inlet, circled every small island—running the wide channels in twos and threes, leaving little mark of their passage. During the summer of 1791, before the arrival of Vancouver's expedition, Spanish vessels had sailed *around* the San Juans, their officers and men viewing the islands from east and west, north and south. But Francisco Eliza's purpose on this expedition was to find the fabled Northwest Passage before any other European power could locate and claim it, so he spared no time for the narrow channels that thread between these massed islands.

Consequently, Lieutenant William Broughton, commanding the *Chatham,* was the first European explorer to see San Juan's Griffin Bay. Captain Vancouver himself was off exploring Puget Sound while his lieutenant undertook a conscientious reconnaissance of the San Juans, as ordered.

Anchoring for the night off Shaw Island (near where today you will see a fleet of Indian-style reef-netters anchored in rows), Broughton divided his force, and the next morning took the *Chatham* through Upright Channel to Harney Channel, sending his two small boats northwestward to explore San Juan Channel. Imagine them: two small vessels, each fifteen to twenty feet long, propelled in solitary grandeur up the channel ahead of you, teams of oarsmen bending to their task.

Except for a few minor struggles with the tides, this first investigation of the route you follow on Cruise Two was uneventful. Woods—above all they saw woods covering almost all of the islands. The natural forests of those days included our much-prized madronas (*Arbutus menziesii,* named for botanist Archibald Menzies who, from his base on Vancouver's *Discovery,* was then examining the shores of Puget Sound). Dogwood, more prevalent on the mainland than on the islands, may well have been in bloom, since this was the month of May, and the native rhododendron would have been out. But mostly they saw fir trees, hemlock, and other conifers clothing the hillsides.

Today, looking up at those same wooded hillsides, you can visualize Broughton's seamen gazing at them, knowing that no one from their part of the world had ever before looked along these shining passages, and wondering, perhaps, if anyone else ever would.

But sixty-seven short years later, the wide scoop of Griffin Bay, just to the south of you, was full of British warships, the *Chatham's* successors on the forward wave of empire. Manned by British sailors and the Royal Marines, they anchored broadside to the shore, their long cannon run out from rows of gunports and trained on a company of U.S. infantry camped on San Juan Island, each man of whom must have been expecting instantaneous annihilation.

The opposing forces were ludicrously out of balance: 5 British warships (*Ganges, Tribune, Pylades, Satellite,* and *Plumper*—167 guns altogether) manned by some 2,000 seamen, gunners, and marines pitted by summer's end against 460 U.S. infantry and artillerymen whose heavy weapons consisted of about 12 cannon mounted on the ridge above the bay. There were hotheads on both sides. James Douglas, governor of the new British colony of Vancouver Island, believed that San Juan Island should be an imperial possession when the disputed international boundary was finally drawn. After all, was it not obvious that a landmass so close to Victoria—scarcely five miles away across Haro Strait—would pose a serious military threat in the hands of a rival power that had already pushed the Hudson's Bay Company from the Columbia River to Vancouver Island?

The American encampment was headed by a Southern officer much given to pushing. Captain George E. Pickett, overwhelmingly outnumbered, was ready to fire on the heavily armed British warships in Griffin Bay. Six years later on the other side of the country, he ordered his outnumbered forces to cross the open valley beneath Cemetery Ridge, in Pickett's Charge on Union forces at Gettysburg. And that, of course, was a disaster for the Confederacy.

But at Griffin Bay there were some cool heads, too. Notable among these was the commanding officer of the Royal Navy, Captain Geoffrey Hornby, who held his fire despite Douglas's directions, until Rear Admiral R. L. Baynes, commander of the Royal Navy in the Pacific, then engaged in open-ocean surveillance in his great man-of-war *Ganges,* could get there. On returning to Victoria, Baynes was shocked at the confrontation of forces in Griffin Bay, and when he learned that it had all come about because an American settler had shot a pig belonging to the Hudson's Bay Company farm, he was even more astounded. The admiral knew that British sovereignty over the island was at stake; nevertheless, he would take no action without direct orders from London. Meanwhile Winfield Scott, the commanding general of the U.S. Army, put leashes around the necks of his two most eagerly combatant subordinates, Captain Pickett and General William S. Harney, in time to prevent the explosion that hovered daily over Griffin Bay during the summer of 1859.

Agreeing at last to a joint military occupation of the island—neither side to land more than one hundred men—both forces lay down their arms, and the Pig War was over. It was twelve years before the German kaiser, called in to mediate the broader question, decided in favor of the United States by running the international boundary down Haro Strait, giving San Juan Island to the United States. Throughout those twelve years, troops remained at American Camp on Griffin Bay and at English Camp on Garrison Bay—at opposite ends of the island.

Today, the two camps make up the San Juan National Historical Park, the only federal historical park on the West Coast that is accessible to pleasure craft. We urge you, at some point in your explorations, to go ashore in Griffin Bay and look around American Camp—if you can manage to anchor in the bay near Fish Creek, which is somewhat exposed to easterlies. Development of American Camp is in progress but not complete at this writing. Improved moorage here will undoubtedly be part of future development plans and will make visiting easier. On this cruise, you will visit English Camp on Garrison Bay instead of American Camp. There a blockhouse and the original barracks that housed British Royal Marines have been restored. With that in mind, perhaps it is time to direct your vessel up San Juan Channel on the first leg of Cruise Two.

Your first stop is San Juan Island's primary town, Friday Harbor, which is no more than ten minutes on power from Turn Island. You will probably approach it in company with a string of boats, interweaving with other strings arriving from other directions. Situated behind Brown Island on a loop of water that opens two ways into San Juan Channel, this thriving town perches on a low bluff. The townsite was particularly appealing to early settlers because of a vigorous spring that poured fresh water in a stream down to this bluff, and it was here they watered their sheep.

The docks of Friday Harbor are alive with boats—coming, going, rafting, shifting slips. On the wide wooden floats people stop to chat, sit at ease in folding chairs, or work on gear. There is vigorous activity at Friday Harbor everywhere you look.

Because it is so close to Fisherman Bay, and even closer to Turn Island, Friday Harbor makes a good breakfast stop for Cruise Two. The well-marked guest docks are on the outer float of the harbor, which gives you a brisk stroll to the ramp that leads up to shore. Once on land, you find yourself in the center of town. Friday Harbor's life-force, its nourishment, pours in through the docks, not primarily from pleasure craft, but from the Anacortes-based ferries that dock here. Long ribbons of parked cars wait between each ferry sailing, and while a ferry is in port, the whole town seems to focus attention on it. So, as you would expect, the streets of Friday Harbor are lined with shops that serve the needs and interests of visitors: an ice-cream parlor, gift shops, restaurants, an inn built and decorated in another day and newly restored for today's guests, and—for the comfort of us boatmen as well as the other visitors—good public rest rooms and showers located in the port office building. If you are low on food, fuel, or ice, Friday Harbor is an excellent port of call.

Unless you have a car or bicycles on San Juan Island, you cannot hope to see the attractive interior of this delightful landfall: the miles of curving country road that ease over the crests of small rolling hills; the cattle ponds winking in shallow ravines; the old and new farm buildings; the lanes bordered so closely by thick woods that they feel like roofless tunnels. But your boat will carry you along the shore, showing you instead a face of the island that is not visible from a car.

If you are like us, navigational matters occupy your mind when you enter a new port for the first time, and these days the main channel into Friday Harbor is so busy that you were probably engaged in keeping clear of traffic, rather than sightseeing, as you approached the town. Besides, if you took our advice and scheduled breakfast in Friday Harbor, while coming in you were undoubtedly hungry, a state that sometimes interferes with one's powers of observation.

Perhaps you can take a moment now as you pull away from this protected harbor to look back and enjoy the charm, the rusticity, and the vigor of this centrally located island town. Roughly one thousand people reside in the one square mile of Friday Harbor. There is a total of twenty-five hundred residents on the fifty-six square miles of San Juan Island, and that means more than a third of its population lives in this town, the only real town on San Juan. It is also the county seat. Two weekly newspapers, the *Friday Harbor Journal* and the *Island Record,* are published here and—together with Eastsound's *Islands' Sounder*—are read all over the San Juans. Published in Friday Harbor since 1906, the *Journal* has had its ups and downs. Once or twice it sank close to dissolution, only to be kept afloat by community enthusiasm and volunteer labor. Today it is thriving. The *Record* is much newer, having been published only for the past three years. Pick up a copy of one or the other of these papers while you are visiting San Juan. They throw a wide, sympathetic light on the special life patterns of the islanders.

Before you leave Friday Harbor, be sure you run eastward along the San Juan shore in the delightfully scenic small passage between San Juan and Brown islands. The shorelines are an unassuming mishmash of waterside business properties, loading docks, small-boat works, and marine ways. There are old buildings, now frankly desolate but reflecting a proud past; rehabilitated residential tugs are tied to piers; a small private yacht basin on Brown Island sports half a dozen sleek vessels. High above the passage, the hillside of San Juan Island shows signs of the excavating and mining activities that have fed the island's economy in the past—gravel here at Bald Hill, and limestone at Roche Harbor, which is our next important destination.

After you have seen your fill, reverse your direction, run through the busy port once more, and set your course to round Point Caution out on San Juan Channel. As you leave Friday Harbor, be sure to notice the handsome building of the University of Washington's oceanographic institute, whose labs are devoted to marine studies of all sorts.

Once you clear the harbor you are ready to run northwestward along an almost unbroken stretch of shoreline. We suggest you stay near San Juan Island for this leg of the cruise, mostly to ensure comfort and relaxed cruising. As you see, San Juan Channel has begun to widen. A long fetch allows winds—particularly our common summertime southeasterlies—to build up both current and chop, so that midchannel can be quite rough. It is exciting if you can hoist sail and soar, drawing all the power you need from the coursing air. This type of following sea is not unpleasant in a powerboat either, but if you like calm water, hug the shore.

You are cruising through the passage that Britain—denied Rosario Channel—much preferred over Haro Strait for the international boundary. Wide open to the north, it looks quite as large from that direction as either of the other two possible water boundaries that were under consideration in the 1860s. But while huge freighters and deep-draft navy vessels ply both Haro and Rosario straits today, not even ferries enter the San Juan Islands through narrow Middle Channel, which is the southernmost exit of San Juan Channel. True, ferries from Anacortes run through Harney Channel and swing south down San Juan Channel on their regular island runs, but they return through Upright Channel and Thatcher Pass. Their regular appearances, like those of the Canadian ferries in the Gulf Islands, are always cheering, even comforting, because they symbolize a denser concentration of humankind located somewhere beyond the wooded hills—far enough away to be out of sight, but near enough to provide aid and succor if needed.

We welcome that comfort, because these are getting to be large waters. Ahead, Flattop and even the much larger Waldron Island are dwarfed by the distant glittering sweep of Haro Strait, flooding into the Strait of Georgia. The Gulf Islands—what we tend to call the northern Gulf Islands to distinguish them from the peppering of small landfalls near Sidney and Swartz Bay—lie off your bow. They are grayed by distance, and their physical features are indistinct. All the near-crowding San Juan Islands seem to have dropped behind to starboard.

It may be with relief that you turn away from so much open water. Rounding Limestone Point, you now alter course westward to run between Spieden Island and San Juan Island, covering the short length of Spieden Channel in a few minutes if under power.

San Juan Island here presents an appealing shoreline, most of it privately owned and distinguished by handsome homes. In contrast, the mounded spine of Spieden looks like something out of the African veld; it is golden with short grasses, crisscrossed by animal trails, and dotted at rare intervals with small clumps of trees.

In the recent past, this look of bare veld prompted some imaginative promoters to establish a big-game preserve on the island, a private hunting ground for safari-hungry marksmen who could afford neither the time nor the money for a trip to genuine big-game country. It was an extraordinary experiment, which, for one reason or another, did not succeed. But for years we ran Spieden Channel with binoculars at our eyes, hoping to glimpse lions, leopards, or rhinos.

You are now approaching one of the most enchanting regions in all the islands, entered through Roche Harbor. A quick glance at the chart of San Juan Island shows you its ragged, much-indented northwest shoulder. Here bays within bays shelter inside Henry Island, giving you much opportunity for quiet, serene boating, for hikes and dinghy explorations, and for impromptu landings. If you are seized with a desire to jump ship here—to abandon Cruise Two, that is—we will understand. Feel free. Or come back another time and spend a week in Roche Harbor, Mosquito Pass, Westcott Bay, Garrison Bay, and Mitchell Bay. Bring your diving gear and go down for abalones, crabs, or octopuses off the shores of Henry Island.

Today our plan is that you make the acquaintance of Roche Harbor, taking care to locate the customs dock, gas dock, grocery store, hotel, tennis courts, swimming pool, bridle trail, and the everywhere-visible remains of those large-scale quarrying operations that brought the first commercial vessels into this harbor.

In the 1880s the hills behind Roche Harbor seemed made of solid limestone, the same kind of rich lime deposits that had been mined near Friday Harbor in the 1860s. John S. McMillin acquired the Roche Harbor lime works in 1886, and a lively town grew up around the enterprise that made McMillin a power in Washington during its first decades of statehood. It was a company town with a company store and an autocratic patriarch who called the tunes until his death in 1936. As the valuable lime deposits at last diminished to a level unprofitable for further working, the town's original economic base faded away. But the fine, Victorian-style buildings remain.

Today, the McMillin home is a first-class restaurant; the Hotel de Haro continues to operate as an attractive "period" hostelry; and the bustling warehouses of the mining company now house lavatories, showers, and laundry facilities for visiting yachtsmen. A popular marine resort draws thousands of pleasure craft to the wharves that once accommodated merchant vessels loading barrels of lime. Recently, Roche Harbor Resort installed a system of mooring buoys to supplement its already long, elaborate floats, and available moorage has thereby been greatly increased.

We always put in for at least one night a summer at Roche Harbor. The open-air swimming pool is large and heated; the dining room, overlooking one of the most attractive seascapes in the islands, serves tasty dinners; and the doughnut shop puts other doughnut shops in the Northwest into the shade.

A short walk along a wooded road brings you to the McMillin family mausoleum, a large, pillared, open-air structure of stone built in the 1930s. Rich in the symbolism of Freemasonry, this memorial

Roche Harbor restaurant on San Juan Island

recalls the McMillin family's practice of spending a peaceful evening hour together seated around the dining table. In the center of a raised floor in the mausoleum is a stone table and a set of six stone chairs. The chairs serve as crypts, where ashes of departed members of the family are deposited. A unique feature of the mausoleum is the set of thirty-foot stone columns, one of which was deliberately broken when installed. The McMillin family explained that the broken column symbolizes the unfinished state of man's labors at the time of death. But among islanders the story persists that it represents the life of a family member who was disowned. Unfortunately the mausoleum has been badly damaged recently by vandals.

We like Roche Harbor's flag-lowering ceremony, held each day at sundown. There is always at least one big sailboat moored in the harbor whose small deck cannon answers the resort's evening gun, and the coupling of American and Canadian anthems is a pleasant reminder of the good border relations both nations have maintained across Haro Strait ever since the Pig War.

For these reasons we have listed Roche Harbor as an optional first-night stop on Cruise Two. However, you have reached Roche Harbor near lunchtime, so if you plan to stay the night here, you should eat, reserve your space with the dock boy, and then take off for an afternoon's jaunt down Mosquito Pass. If you have had enough of busy harbors, you can plan instead to anchor for the night in Garrison Bay, just off the pass.

Mosquito Pass is used by many yachtsmen as a convenient shortcut to Victoria. About two miles long, it opens out of Roche Harbor to the south through a slim passage that looks, at first glance, like a dead end. After a short southerly leg, however, the channel bends sharply westward, requiring you to go around tiny Pole Island, which you take to starboard. Mosquito Pass then loops widely against Henry Island, and throughout its length you will want to be on the lookout for divers' flags because this is a favorite underwater spot.

Midway, the port shoreline opens between two prominent bluffs and invites you to probe still farther inland. You can see the broad expanse of Westcott Bay through this opening, and as you enter it a second haven—Garrison Bay—opens to the south. These waters are tucked well inland and are all but completely landlocked. Twice-protected from the racing currents of Haro Strait, they rise and fall with the tides but are otherwise very still. All you need worry about in these two bays is the water depth near the innermost shores. A lead line will come in handy if you spend the night, and be sure to double-check the tide tables on minimum depths.

We spent a recent summer's night in Garrison Bay, anchored— we thought—over the three-quarter fathom line. It was a night of meteor showers and we reclined on the bow, watching the skies from dusk until midnight. No bright dock lights lessened the blackness against which those dots of brilliant light streaked. Afterward, we slept soundly, but at dawn the eel grasses were bent against the chine of our boat, and we hurriedly moved our anchor to deeper water.

Garrison Bay tells the other half of the Pig War story that began in Griffin Bay in 1859. By agreement, the British Royal Marines—some eighty-nine men—were landed near an enormous broad-leaved maple, which still stands at the edge of a meadow on Garrison Bay's east shore. In tents at first, then in neat rows of wooden buildings, the men "occupied" the island. Working in harmony with their American counterparts from the other end of San Juan, they helped keep order on this raw frontier and— incidentally—did a little lime quarrying themselves. They built a fortified blockhouse, which you will see restored on the shore of the bay, and used it to discourage marauding war parties of northern

Blockhouse at English Camp on San Juan Island

Indian tribesmen, primarily Haidas.

They planted a small, formal English garden (was someone homesick?), built officers' houses, and eventually, as the need arose, laid out a cemetery on the hill.

Part of the story that appeals to us has to do with the height of the trees that crowd the shore of Garrison Bay. Land rises and dips on all sides, climbing at one point to the modest height of Young Hill (680 feet), which overlooks the east-bank meadow. All these mounds and hills, even the mountain itself, are bristled with tall Douglas firs and other evergreens. It is as if the land wore a stiff, well-combed beard. But to the west, where in a small saddle the ground rises only slightly higher than sea level, there is a swathe of short trees. It looks like a single cut of a lawn mower through a patch of high grass.

Legend has it that this stand of short trees—this window through the woods—is here because the British wanted a line of vision from English Camp to Haro Strait, just where Mosquito Pass opens to the south. Trees along this line were felled and seedlings removed by order of the English commander, so that he could see vessels as they approached from Victoria or up the coast of San Juan Island. While any ships—early steamboats as well as sail—negotiated the southern half of Mosquito Pass and swung through the narrows into Garrison Bay, the garrison itself could be making ready for inspection or, if need be, for defense. They were never caught unprepared.

If you decide to spend the night in Garrison Bay, be sure to go ashore and inquire about the programs that may be scheduled in the historical park during your stay. They are many and various, including period songfests, dancefests, discussions of regional geology, botany, and assorted marine sciences. Most are held in the restored barracks, and a visit ashore is more evocative of life a hundred years ago than any number of historical films.

Amenities in the park are limited, however. Consult the bulletin board on the side of the barracks for regulations and up-to-date information about fishing, clamming, and picnicking. There is no water in the park, and fires of all kinds are forbidden. If you like, you can write ahead for information to: Superintendent, San Juan Island National Historical Park, Box 549, Friday Harbor, Washington 98250.

Mornings in the islands are so peaceful that we always take our time over a galley breakfast. It is usually after ten before we raise the anchor or release our mooring lines. We assume you will want to do the same.

On this second day of Cruise Two you will emerge—when you are ready—into a wide-open body of water, just outside the entrance to Roche Harbor. If you spent the night in Garrison Bay, you have only to retrace your course northward up Mosquito Pass, then cross directly to the western mouth of Roche Harbor.

Your destination this morning is Turn Point, on the westernmost tip of Stuart Island. Turn Point is also the westernmost tip of the San Juan archipelago; beyond it to the west and north are Canadian waters and Canadian islands, just over that invisible line drawn in 1872. This leg of Cruise Two is less scenic than challenging. Haro

Strait, galloping along to port, is fairly wide here. Across it you can see Sidney Island and a myriad of small mounds and humps that mark the southern Gulf Islands. Spieden Island to starboard looks farther away than the chart suggests. And in all probability you have some fog. If so, you must take whatever precautions you deem appropriate. We have encountered much fog in this particular stretch of water, but only once was it dense enough to make us rely on our compass alone.

A vague outline of the island you are heading for usually is visible through the mist. If not, you can strike a line due north (true north) and proceed cautiously until the shore of Stuart Island is visible, then follow it to Turn Point.

Turn Point is marked by a lighthouse on the bluff above the shore. Like all such installations, it has a peculiar beauty, one that is derived from more than the shape of some small structures whose exotic profiles are outlined against a tip of land—always a tip of land, thrust out into the sea. Perhaps the beauty is related to a skipper's knowledge that danger lurks where the great lights stand, that here is civilization pitted against the wilder forces of nature, or even that here is evidence of man's occasional humanity to man. In any case, Turn Point marks tide rips that fan out toward the central channel of Haro Strait (which, you will note on the chart, "turns" here). You would do well to circle out around these rips, heading for the area where the strait's surface changes from foam-tipped ridges to more normal-looking chop.

Swing back eastward from Turn Point, and run the short distance to Prevost Harbor, which is suggested as your second night's moorage on Cruise Two. Prevost Harbor is one of Washington's most popular marine parks, for many excellent reasons. Like Friday Harbor, it is a deep, C-shaped indentation on the northeast face of an island. Little Satellite Island (privately owned—trespassers repelled) lies inside the "C," blocking winds and currents from the northeast. The southeasterlies and occasional strong westerlies do not disturb the calm of this superb haven. Its eastern opening is rocky, narrow, and shallow. Most skippers use the western entrance, being careful even there to watch for rocks, reefs, and kelp. Once inside, you can pick the kind of moorage you like best, particularly if you arrive shortly after noon, as is likely.

There is room for a few boats at floats attached to the long elevated dock at Prevost Harbor State Park. A row of buoys offers additional moorage, and anchorage is good either near the park or across the harbor by Satellite Island. The water in Prevost Harbor usually lies flat as a mirror. We have explored all parts of it in our dinghy and allowed our daughter—from age six on—to row back and forth across it alone, as often as she liked.

A heavily wooded but narrow saddle on Stuart Island forms the landward section of the park and joins Prevost Harbor State Park to Reid Harbor State Park on the south side of Stuart. The bulk of Stuart Island is privately owned, with a small residential population; only this belt connecting the two park harbors is public property. Though small, the land area is equipped for camping and picnicking, has pit toilets and trash disposal bins, and offers fine views from a number of good trails. Beachcombing, wading, birding, and photography are all rewarding at Prevost.

Or you can simply stand beneath the tall trees and look out between their dark, mossy boles at the flash and gleam of distant waters, the curved sails of approaching yachts, and the mass of white cumulus suds piled against a distant horizon. Aren't you glad you stopped at Prevost?

Cruise Three departs from Prevost Harbor, so turn now to Cruise Three if you propose to link the two cruises. If you must head back, however, the return course for Cruise Two lies along the flank of Stuart Island, with your compass reading a little south of east. On a fine morning you will be heading into the sun, wearing dark glasses against the glitter of the water. Passing north of Flattop Island, you cross President Channel on a more southerly angle and watch the fir mound of Jones Island gradually separate itself from the high mass of Orcas. Jones is your destination—another state marine park boasting two small harbors, one north, one south.

Please do stop at Jones Island, even if it is too early for lunch. You are more than halfway back to Turn Island and should be able to afford the time for an exploratory midday break in your cruise. Again, the north harbor is the best protected. It has several buoys, a small pier with floats capable of accommodating about six boats, and a basin large enough to hold perhaps ten more boats riding at anchor. Beginning at the pier and running through deep woods, a root-roughened path leads across the small island to the south side where three mooring buoys mark the more open and exposed inlet. Other small coves and bights on the south shore sometimes host a vessel or two at anchor, although the location makes for a rocky night's sleep and is not recommended.

A raised meadow standing like a balcony above these southern coves has a large fire pit for campers and a scattering of old apple trees, remnants of an ancient orchard. If you stand quite still and peer back into the woods that edge this meadow, you will see cautiously moving or motionless shapes, tan-colored, with flashes of white here and there. Break off a leafy twig from an apple tree and hold it out, moving as little as possible and saying nothing. Presently they begin to

Prevost Harbor on Stuart Island

emerge—one or two of the more-tame-than-wild Jones Island deer. They love apple tree leaves. You hold one end of the branch, and small teeth beneath large brown suspicious eyes will tug at the other. How many deer are there? It is hard to tell. If you walk the path after dark, a doe may precede you in the shadows, keeping pace at a distance, sometimes with a spotted fawn at her side. We have never counted more than eight in sight at one time, but who knows how many the woods hide? They are protected from hunters because Jones is a wildlife preserve.

We like to anchor in the north cove even though its weedy bottom sometimes makes the hook reluctant to hold. At sundown on our last visit, we watched the smooth water reflect those incredible amethyst, opal, and mother-of-pearl shades and followed with our eyes the minute V-shaped paths etched fleetingly by the pricklebacks, whose heads just barely broke the surface of our little harbor.

No doubt you will come back to Jones for an overnight stay—almost everyone does. It has picnic tables, barbecue grills, water, twenty-one camping sites, and a number of hiking trails that lead around the circumference of its 179 acres.

From Jones you embark on the last leg of a cruise shaped like a bent paper clip. You leave your moorage by way of Spring Passage—a broad, well-traveled lane between Jones and the imposing flank of Orcas, which is the largest of the San Juan Islands. Cruise Four circles Orcas, so we need say no more here than that Steep Point and Spring Passage mark its southwesternmost extremity. Steep Point towers above you as you head on down the eastern side of San Juan Channel.

Before reaching Shaw Island and waters made familiar by the first stage of this cruise, you will pass either beside or through the beautiful cluster of small, rounded landfalls known collectively as the Wasp Islands. If you have time, perhaps you should nose through them, watching for rocks and shallows as you remember another dramatic era of the past. These were the islands that sheltered famous smuggling gangs in the prohibition days of the 1920s. Imagine: silent hulls, drifting along these channels, propelled by muffled oars or fragments of sail—slipping, as if by magic, out of the pursuing revenue officers' sight. Encampments and rendezvous spots and hurried flights enlivened the Wasps in those days, however tranquil they look today.

Now you have a direct run back to your starting point, a half hour on power, and Cruise Two, the evocative "historical" run, is over. Other cruises in this book stop briefly at San Juan Island, primarily for the convenience of the customs dock. But you have seen enough to know that a whole summer could be spent savoring this one historic landmass.

Your homeward course from Cruise Two is up to you, and the location of your home port will probably determine it. Will you spend another night near the junction of San Juan and Upright channels or stop somewhere else along the way? Indian Cove on Shaw Island is well worth exploring as a possible stop. The beach is beautiful white sand, much of it is a county park, and it is a pleasant place to wade or build sand castles. Temporary anchorage here is good, but the cove is exposed to southwest winds and—depending on the weather—may not be trustworthy overnight. Parks Bay, to the southwest behind Point George, is a secure overnight anchorage—one where the sunsets are often spectacular.

Another possible stop is across East Sound from Shaw Island. This is the village of Olga, which is perched on an Orcas Island bluff from which a flight of stairs leads down to a tiny but convenient set of floats on the sound below. It is a gloriously picturesque spot. The floats are within walking distance of the Chambered Nautilus, one of the islands' most distinguished restaurants. If your boat's chef has cooked as many galley meals, straight running, as he or she can endure, Olga may be the place for you.

Cruise

Three

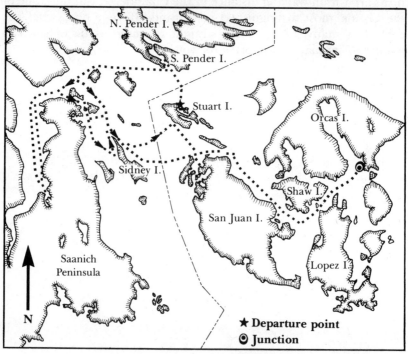

Do not use for navigation.
Use NOAA 18423, Folio Small-Craft Chart, and Canadian Hydrographic
Service Small Craft Chart 3310

Stuart Island to Butchart Gardens

Point of departure: Prevost Harbor on Stuart Island

Course: across Haro Strait to South Pender Island, Canada; then via Swanson Channel, Satellite Channel, Saanich Inlet, Tod Inlet; return via Shute or Colburne passages, Sidney Channel, Miners Channel, Haro Strait, San Juan Channel, Upright Channel to East Sound

Stops: Bedwell Harbour (Canadian Customs), Brentwood Bay, Butchart Gardens, Sidney Spit, Roche Harbor or Friday Harbor (U.S. Customs)

Length of cruise: approximately 51 nautical miles to Roche Harbor; 69 nautical miles to junction with Cruise Four

Duration on power: 3 to 4 days

Duration on sail: 3 to 6 days

Overnight moorage:
First night: Brentwood Bay or Tod Inlet
Second night: Sidney Spit

Junction point for Cruise Four: vicinity of Obstruction Pass (Olga, Rosario Resort, Obstruction Pass Boating Area, or Blakely Marina)

A Garden Cruise

We have mentioned that Prevost Harbor is much loved, for many excellent reasons. One of these is its location, farther to the north and west than any other overnight moorage in the San Juans. Because of this position, Prevost Harbor makes an ideal jumping-off place for a cruise into Canadian waters. Cruise Three takes you to Butchart Gardens on Vancouver Island. It covers a substantial distance—almost all of it in Canada—so you will not want to linger too long over breakfast in your Prevost Harbor moorage, pleasant though it may be. Be sure that your galley is well stocked with finger-food items for the day's run: cheese and crackers, fruit and cookies, cold sandwiches. Since there are not many convenient lunch stops en route, you will want to eat as you cruise.

Emerging from Prevost Harbor, you will find yourself facing Haro Strait, and your course lies almost directly across it. North and slightly west of Stuart Island, beyond the striped surface of Haro, you will see an island marked by a conical hill; head for that hill (Mount Norman) on South Pender Island. It took us some summers to realize that every time we needed to clear customs at Bedwell Harbour we were heading for that particular hill. Bedwell Harbour lies just beneath it, cutting deep into South Pender Island. The stripes you must cross to reach it will turn out to be variations in the water surface of Haro Strait—some of them tide rips, some crisscrossed wakes, some current and wind patterns cut in this open expanse of water. Sometimes the crossing can be rather choppy, other times as smooth as glass. Fortunately, this is one of the shortest distances across Haro Strait, and it will not be long before you are passing around the claw-shaped rocks of Peter Cove and putting into Bedwell. While you cross the strait, keep a lookout for killer whales. These sleek, beautiful, black and white creatures of the sea often move up and down Haro Strait, sometimes singly, sometimes in pods. If luck is with you, you may be treated to the sight of one or more breaking through the water in great porpoiselike leaps.

Enter Bedwell Harbour midchannel if the traffic allows, and head directly for the Canadian customs dock on your right. Since you will have occasion to clear both U.S. and Canadian customs a number of times in following the various border-boating cruises outlined in this book, we have made suggestions about how to do it in the "Crossing the Line" chapter. There is one unexpected pleasure about the procedure you might notice now. In contrast to crossing the border on the mainland highways, marked as they often are in summer months by long lines of irritated drivers who tend to snap at the customs officers (and are occasionally snapped at in return by those same much-tried souls), a border crossing in the islands is low-key and easy going, with amiable smiles all around. See if you don't think so!

Spend little time in Bedwell Harbour this morning; you will be coming back again. And now the gardens are calling. So head back out of the harbor, around Wallace Point on the southwest, and set a westward course across Swanson Channel and then southwestward into Satellite Channel, which flows between Salt Spring Island and Saanich Peninsula. Your course now lies through Satellite Channel and down Saanich Inlet to the south.

What is the best route across Swanson Channel? The weather will help you decide. If it is fair, with light winds and glassy waters, and if you are lucky enough to have neither haze nor fog, just set forth, keeping Moresby and Portland islands to port and cutting a little south of midchannel through Satellite Channel.

If, on the other hand, you have overcast skies threatening rain, or a wind-driven chop, or perhaps drifts of fog, you may prefer to hug the coast of South Pender Island until you reach the navigation light set on a white pillar, just south of Mouat Point. From here you can easily see the corresponding light, on another white pillar, that marks Beaver Point on Salt Spring Island. We have crossed Swanson Channel at this point, with the aid of these two highly visible lights, even in a fairly dense fog, but it is better, of course, if you can cruise on bright clear days and enjoy sun and scenery. If you choose this second crossing, you can follow the Salt Spring shore all the way from Beaver Point to Satellite Channel. Admittedly, this is the long way around and it involves crossing the mouth of busy Fulford Harbour, but it will take you where you want to go, and you will not have to rely exclusively on compass headings.

One caveat for the next leg of the cruise to Butchart Gardens: Saanich Inlet traps a substantial amount of driftwood, and fast-moving power craft will want to maintain a continuous watch for floating and submerged logs.

Moses Point on Saanich Peninsula is marked offshore by Wain Rock, and your course lies around the rock, then south. You may find yourself zigzagging a bit at this point, however direct the ideal course lies. Fishing is excellent where Saanich Inlet waters mingle with those of Satellite Channel, and the water may be literally dancing with fishing boats. Some will be commercial vessels but most are pleasure craft. If you find such activity tempting, remember that you cannot fish in Canadian waters without a special license for your boat, and the time to buy one, if at all possible, is *before* you set out to cross the border. Lacking that license, you are constrained to thread a cautious path between or around the intent fishermen, watching salmon jump on lines that bend their poles into tight arcs.

Beyond this favored spot, you cross the wide-open mouth of Patricia Bay, which is used by the Canadian navy and banned to pleasure craft. Saanich Inlet is very wide at this point, and the land behind Patricia Bay lies low. Brisk easterlies can sweep without hindrance across the waters you are now traversing. Depending on your type of vessel, the next fifteen minutes will be either delightful (on a sailboat) or bumpy (on a small, planing hull), but once you reach the lee of Yarrow Point, the chop should lessen noticeably.

Like a fjord, the big funnel of water increases in beauty as you reach the narrow stretches nearer its head. In the distance, mountains loom high above the little town of Bamberton and close in like canyon walls on either side of Squally Reach. Surrounded by the deep hunter-green of our northwestern forests, you slow down to run be-tween little Senanus Island and Hagan Bight and enter Brentwood Bay. For the first time since leaving Bedwell Harbour, you find yourself cruising along a built-up waterfront. Above it, strung out along a low bluff to port, is the colorful Brentwood Bay community, which appears to bristle with docks. A number of hazardous rocks lie in Brentwood Bay, and only some of them are well marked. At low tide, especially, you will want to proceed with caution. Some unmarked reefs stand close to the surface.

Brentwood Bay is right around a modest point of land from Butchart Gardens, and you may wish to arrange your night's moorage before going on. Four separate marinas offer transient yachtsmen moorage and a variety of amenities. At the end of its main pier, one marina displays a large sign that reads "Daily Moorage." This is the Brentwood Inn, where we usually stay. It has a good restaurant and a friendly pub with a wide deck overlooking the bay.

From Brentwood Bay you enter Tod Inlet, which opens to the south. Turn immediately to port once in the inlet and then enter Butchart Gardens' small but deep natural harbor, which is walled in shining stone and is well protected. Here a small courtesy dock accommodates about eight boats. If you wish to stay the night here rather than in Brentwood Bay, put down your anchor a short way out from the dock. The bottom is good and you can stay until morning. If you tie to the dock you will be required to move off at midnight, by

Anchorage by dock of Butchart Gardens on Vancouver Island

which time the anchorage will be crowded. Our method is to anchor off the dock when we first arrive, dinghy to the dock, see the gardens, dine in the restaurant that was once the Butchart family home, stay for the exquisitely beautiful evening program, then dinghy back to the boat and turn in. If possible, try to arrange your cruise so as to avoid this stop on a summer weekend.

Given the limited moorage at the gardens, you might ask why we chose Butchart Gardens for a cruise destination. After a visit there you will no longer wonder. Butchart Gardens is simply one of those places one goes, like the Tuileries in Paris, Princes Gardens in Edinburgh, or the Shalimar Gardens in Lahore. You do not need to live in the Northwest to know about them. People come from all over the globe to enjoy their astonishing beauty.

The site was a working limestone quarry at the end of the last century. The limestone gave out eventually, leaving a hole in the ground—huge, unsightly, even dangerous; it was located a short distance from the home of the quarry's owner, Robert Pim Butchart, an early Canadian industrialist who specialized in the manufacture of Portland cement.

If a worked-out quarry disfigured the grounds on which your home stood, would you elect to mask it with an enormous flower garden? Butchart's wife made that decision. Today you can stand on the rim of the old quarry and look down onto banks blazing with color, dense flower walls that edge velvet lawns and curving brick walks. The sides of the quarry support a many-toned greenness of shrubs and trees. Fountains leap high into the air without topping its rim. But the flower gardens have long since spilled over the top and run down to the sea at Tod Inlet.

A sloping, tree-shaded path above your anchorage leads up the side of the cliff to a delicate Japanese garden, first of the group of gardens that you will explore in your gradual climb toward the rambling Butchart home at the top of the slope above the cliff. Here dwarf trees, pools, tiny bridges, and miniature terraces fill a triangle of land. To the left above the Japanese garden is the star pond and the Italian garden, with its tall Lawson cypress, its fountain, and its statuary. To the right, along curving walkways edged in riotous bloom, is the formal rose garden, planted English-fashion around a circle of grass. In between these two arms stretches the flawless lawn, striped with the marks of a mower into two shades of green, a perfect foil for the old home. As you dine here, you look out over the gardens and glimpse in the distance the bit of water where your boat rides at anchor. At night you may see a Scottish tattoo, puppets, or a variety show, and you will surely walk amazed among the brilliantly lighted fountains and grottoes.

We will assume a late-morning departure from Tod Inlet or Brentwood Bay. Until you reach Moses Point you merely retrace your course, so perhaps the glow of the previous evening may be permitted to linger that long. But as you round Moses Point into Satellite Channel, you will want to look at your chart.

Your second destination on Cruise Three is Sidney Spit Marine Park, and the simplest way to reach it is to head east through Satellite Channel, southeast down Shute Passage, then south between Forrest and Dock islands. But this is not the most scenic route. If, like us, you enjoy inside passages, near views of tiny hidden coves, and the shifting shapes of small, densely firred islands to left and right, try threading Colburne Passage.

Your first landmark on this route is tiny Arbutus Island. You cannot miss it: it is nothing but a small mound of earth supporting a single tree. Even from a distance you can identify the tree as a madrona, the *Arbutus menziesii* described by Vancouver's botanist in 1792. There is an artistic integrity about the sight: a miniature island, named Arbutus, bearing one tree in classic proportion. No wonder this scene is so often painted and photographed.

Running midchannel between Arbutus Island and the shore of Saanich Peninsula, you enter busy Colburne Passage. This is a beautiful stretch of water, made lively by the maneuvering of ferries putting in to Swartz Bay. Workboats, channel dredgers, fishing boats, yachts, ferries, and tiny sailboats all use this channel, most of them simultaneously. You simply throttle down and crawl through. If you are sail driven, it is time to reduce your sail surface and perhaps engage the auxiliary. In the confined space of Colburne, the giant ferries cannot maneuver; small-craft skippers must stay out of their way.

Beyond the ferry docks, you will find two channels opening to starboard, one on either side of little Goudge Island. The first, westernmost passage runs by attractive Canoe Bay and is full of small islands and rocks. The second, or easternmost, is narrow but relatively clear of impediments. You can see all the way through it. This is John Pass (or John Passage), and—if you do not know the Canoe Bay area—we suggest you try John Pass first.

Our initial experience of John Pass gave us one of our more vivid boating memories. All three of us had taken up good watch positions, because when you are heading south a shallow patch forms a hazard to port about halfway through the pass, and rocks lie off the starboard point of land as you emerge from the passage. Day beacons mark both danger spots, and the passage between them—while very narrow—is no problem, even for strangers—except, of course, that we met a boat coming through the other way. John Pass was obviously familiar water for the other skipper, but we felt a little as if we were trying to pass a car on a one-way bridge, only here Bill could not slow down without losing his two or three knots of control over the helm. We passed without scraping paint, and the other skipper gave us a cheerful wave. Suddenly we were in open water at the mouth of Tsehum Harbour.

By the time you win free to this same open water, between Tsehum Harbour and Little Shell Island, you will be surrounded by islands—large, small, rocky, tree covered. Among them runs a silver tracery of channels that lies like lace off the inner face of Vancouver Island. Ahead, on the big island's shore, is the port town of Sidney. A round basin of clear blue water edges the hillside on which Sidney perches, and it also is rimmed by clusters and dots of islands. Busy small-boat traffic draws cobweb patterns across this basin; a dozen sails show white against the dark green of James Island; small in the distance, another slim, white triangle approaches up Miners Channel. And again, at regular intervals, the vast bulk of an arriving or departing ferry makes the small craft look like toys.

Directly across this basin is your destination for tonight, Sidney Spit Marine Park. Largest of the nearby landfalls, Sidney Island lifts a tall ridge over its long sandspit and rises in its broader, thicker southeastern end to a solid mound over Hughes Passage. The island has a distinctive geological history that it shares with few others in the Gulf Island group. It was formed when glaciers of the Ice Age deposited a huge mound of sand, gravel, and boulders here. When the ice retreated the mound was left, in something like its present form, to be

Olga on Orcas Island

further molded by winds, rain, and tides, down to the present day.

The park consists of the spit itself and a small section of the elevated ridge adjoining it. At low tide, when the thread of sand adds fine beaches to both its sides, the island looks like a crouched animal with a long, broken tail. The crest of the spit, golden with sea grasses in the sunshine, supports a fretwork of silvery driftwood. When the tide rises, water washes over most of the spit, which is then visible as a row of pilings—a gap-toothed comb that warns skippers to go around. The outermost tip of the spit is marked by a large, very visible light.

There is a small public float on the side of Sidney Spit that faces Vancouver Island. It is convenient for temporary tie-ups, but you are not supposed to moor there for the night. Mooring buoys line the beach, and the bottom is excellent for anchoring. Ashore, you can sunbathe, wade, and swim. There are campsites laid out on the part of the park that stretches along the tree-covered ridge. Drinking water, toilets, trash containers—all are provided without sacrificing the impression of unhampered nature that characterizes this beautiful British Columbia marine park.

From the deck of your boat, you watch the light die over Vancouver Island, maybe in a spectacular, flaming sunset; later the lights of Sidney wink on against the land's black silhouette. Friendly Canadian yachtsmen on neighboring boats are obviously enjoying the good life: singing, joking, or just watching the long parade of boats into Sidney Harbour across the water.

Morning will see you on the way home. You cannot complete this cruise by returning to Prevost Harbor, because your first stateside stop must be at a U.S. customs dock. You can either run down Miners Channel northeast of Sidney Island, and cross directly from there to Roche Harbor or thread your way between the lovely small islands to the north, including Domville and Gooch, to cross Haro Strait near Turn Point. From there you avoid the larger waves of Haro Strait by hugging Stuart Island's shore southward, crossing near the tip of Spieden into Roche Harbor. Having left Sidney Spit fairly early, you may decide not to stop at Roche at all, but to return down San Juan Channel to Friday Harbor's customs station. If you choose to follow Cruise Four, you will want to go from here through Upright Channel to East Sound and settle in for the night at Obstruction Pass Boating Area, at the popular resort of Rosario on Cascade Bay (for which, in the summer, you will need reservations), at the slim little dock of Olga, or at Blakely Marina on Peavine Pass (reservations advised).

Cruise
Four

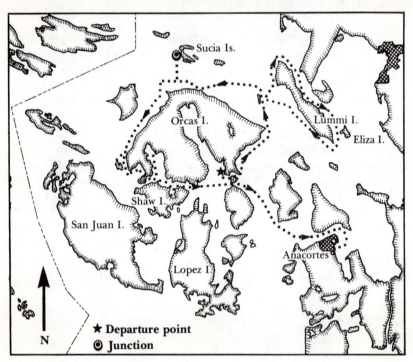

Sucia Is.

Orcas I.

Lummi I.

Eliza I.

Shaw I.

San Juan I.

Lopez I.

Anacortes

★ Departure point
◉ Junction

N

Do not use for navigation.
Use NOAA 18423, Folio Small-Craft Chart

All around Orcas,
and Lummi, Too

Point of departure: the west side of Obstruction Pass

Course: via Obstruction Pass, Rosario Channel, Hale Passage, President Channel, Spring Passage, Deer Harbor, Pole Pass, West Sound, Harney Channel, East Sound, Peavine Pass; return down Rosario Strait to Guemes Channel and Anacortes

Stops: Clark Island, Village Point, Bartel's Resort, Deer Harbor, Blind Island, Olga

Length of cruise: approximately 57 nautical miles back to departure point, or 68 nautical miles to Anacortes

Duration on power: 3 days

Duration on sail: 3 to 5 days

Overnight moorage:

First night: Clark Island State Marine Park, Sucia Islands, or Bartel's Resort

Second night: Deer Harbor Resort or Blind Island State Marine Park

This ends "The San Juans and Saanich." To begin Cruise Five, set a course for the Sucia Islands, approximately 13 nautical miles northwest of Obstruction Pass.

The Mountain Cruise

Orcas Island lifts steep shoulders all around East Sound. Closing ranks to north and west, the great bluffs crowd the waters at their feet, shading them early in the afternoon. Black against the setting sun, they draw in brisk winds to comb the sound with white foam and herringbone. A boat can bounce on the chop in their shadow—with night on one shore and evening on the other—while above the westward-facing bluff still blazes with sunlight, and south beyond Diamond Point the wide basin of East Sound shimmers like a pond.

If you have just come from Cruise Three, East Sound will remind you of Saanich Inlet where it narrows toward Finlayson Arm. Prompted by Saanich to think of fjords (and perhaps of dragon-headed Viking ships), you will find East Sound even more enchanted, even more evocative of polar mists and Norse gods. Long-forgotten sagas may thrum down to you from the dark masses of fir and cedar and hemlock.

Cruise Four assumes you will be ready to set out after breakfast on a three- to five-day circuit of Orcas and Lummi islands. To do so, you will have to spend the previous night somewhere inside or west of Obstruction Pass, probably in East Sound. Where will you find that moorage?

The town of Eastsound, serenely at rest above the innermost reaches of the fjord, has been slow to provide accommodation for visiting yachtsmen. Plans on various drawing boards include a municipal marina, but until it materializes you will have to choose among the following: the luxury resort of Rosario overlooking Cascade Bay, the town dock of Olga to the south and east of Rosario, the parklike boating area at the entrance of Obstruction Pass, or Blakely Marina just south of Obstruction Island on Peavine Pass.

Here are some thoughts to help you make a choice.

Rosario is the best-known resort in the San Juan Islands. In what was once the residence of Robert Moran, a Seattle industrialist and ex-mayor, it offers the comfort of a superb hotel, a good dining room, a gift shop, and indoor and outdoor pools. Fine carved woods, spacious windows, and pleasing proportions characterize the rooms of the old mansion, while along the bluff a number of new two-unit apartments add to the available accommodations.

Yachtsmen frequently book these elegant amenities, but as often as not, they are content to moor at Rosario's sheltered floats, sleep aboard or in one of the modest boatel units near the dock, and eat from their own galleys or lunch lightly in the small dockside coffee shop. Recently, as Rosario has come to enjoy increasing patronage from all over the Northwest, the resort has instituted a system of minimum charges. When you moor at the marina, you must purchase a book of scrip, which is good at all of the resort's facilities. But yachtsmen having no desire to book a room and no interest in an elaborate dinner may find themselves paying a high price for moorage alone.

A less expensive night can be spent at Olga's dock. It is nearby and charges only a modest fee for moorage at its floats, which can accommodate about sixteen boats. Olga, on Buck Bay, is a small, friendly community of about sixty-five families. The stairway at the head of the pier leads up to the main street of the village and to the Chambered Nautilus Restaurant, with its outstanding international cuisine.

Obstruction Pass Boating Area is south of Olga and just a bit east, at the entrance to the pass itself. It has a few mooring buoys and good anchorage close to shore, out of the currents of the pass. The park has campsites, picnic tables, fireplaces, and pit toilets but no local water supply as yet. Its attractive little beach and its woods are pleasant places for leisurely strolls.

Our final alternative, Blakely Marina, is to the south at Peavine Pass and provides comfortable, sheltered moorage and a small grocery store, together with showers and laundry facilities. But since it is crowded in summer, reservations are advised.

If you stay at either Olga or the boating area, we wish you the kind of sunsets that always seem to close our days at these spots. Flaming bars of orange and scarlet stand out against a pale lettuce sky, while across the broad sweep of water from Harney Channel to Lopez Sound bands of opal and gold shine as if the sun's light were rising through the waters from below. Dividing brilliant sky from incandescent water, the narrow black outlines of the distant islands rise: Upright Head like a great thumb in the center, Humphrey Head beside it to the east, and Shaw Island lying low to the west. A ferry cuts its shining forked wake from Thatcher Pass out of the south. Birds flash like black slivers against the golden air, and you will toy again with the idea of living here, year around.

Robert Moran did more than toy with the idea. A self-made and wealthy man, he was still young when he developed a heart condition that forced him to sell his business enterprises in Seattle and move to

Orcas Island for his health. He was not expected to live long. Perhaps Orcas possessed some revitalizing serenity. In any case, Moran lived for forty more years, retired, on Orcas. It makes you think, doesn't it?

In the morning, ready for Cruise Four, you set out eastward through Obstruction Pass. The Orcas shore of this short, busy channel, bent like a camel's back to the north, is lined with gracious, recently constructed homes that are obviously year-round residences.

Two centuries ago, long before anyone thought of building houses here, Lieutenant William Broughton took the *Chatham* through this same pass, after discovering and exploring the inner San Juan waters. The deep water against Obstruction Island would have given him no trouble, but the sweep to port must have been both a hazard and a temptation, then as now. Winds in the pass are freaky, and Broughton's sailors may well have had to fight their sheets on that first voyage through.

Deer Point, to port as you leave Obstruction Pass, is a rocky promontory, parting currents and tidal waters that flow from several different directions. The water surface beyond it is likely to present a broad patch of tide rips, not unlike those off Turn Point on Stuart Island. Here, however, the racing waters seem to attract fish runs. You will find yourself emerging into a cluster of small boats, most of them moving slowly on power, trailing lines, crisscrossing between Lydia Shoal and Deer Point. Our practice (unless we ourselves are fishing) is to circle around them at four or five knots, making little wake, before we head north along the Orcas shoreline.

From this point, Cruise Four describes a figure eight, one loop being substantially smaller than the other. You stay near Orcas Island from Deer Point to Point Lawrence, then cross Rosario Strait by way of Clark Island and Village Point on Lummi Island. Looping north around Point Migley, you run southeast along the entire northeastern face of Lummi Island, then double back around Carter Point, and recross Rosario Strait just south of Lummi Rocks.

You cannot avoid being aware of the sheer bulk of Orcas as you begin the first leg of this cruise. The island spreads like a great cape over the top of the San Juans. It has many hills and knobs, ridges and cliffs. And directly above you, as you coast comfortably along this outflung edge, rises the proud mass of Mount Constitution—2,454 feet high, the tallest uplift in the archipelago. The central peak and diminishing shoulders of this mountain occupy most of Orcas to the east of East Sound. As a result, population here is sparse. The undulating lowlands and bluffs between Deer Point and Point Lawrence rise gradually until they reach a sharp incline that lifts to Mountain Lake, which is halfway to the top of the mountain. Above

Cougar at Doe Bay on Orcas Island

the clear, cold waters of this high-rise lake, the peak thrusts suddenly skyward a thousand feet, almost straight up.

Near at hand there are many rocks and islets lying against the big island's shore, including tiny, wooded Doe Island, which is a convenient, popular state marine park. You will see more of Doe Island if you follow Cruise Eleven.

Close by is Doe Bay, once the most popular rendezvous for island boatmen. Now privately owned, it no longer has facilities for visiting yachtsmen. If you are exploring close in to shore, however, you may see a carved wooden cougar standing on a low bluff above Doe Bay. Ears back, eyes wide, the watchful beast seems to challenge the winds of Rosario Strait.

The low bluff is a mile or more long. Along its rim, half hidden in trees, a sprinkling of houses faces outward to the water. Beyond them, buildings are few and isolated.

Fishermen troll this entire stretch of coastline so you will have company at least as far as Point Lawrence, and the increasing wildness of the land will not leave you friendless in a wet Shangri-la.

Before you reach the point, the treeless, beguiling Peapods lift their small grassy meadows out of the waters ahead, marking a chain of large rocks and tiny islets that have trapped many an unwary skipper. "To get hung up on the Peapods" was one of the first hazards we heard about in these waters; we suggest you describe a generous circle around them. With luck, as you pass you will see a herd of seals sunning on the Peapod grasses or among the broken rocks of their shores; if even luckier, you will see the exotic tufted puffin swimming just offshore.

Rounding Point Lawrence, you can look northwestward along the most isolated, most abrupt stretch of Orcas Island's long shoreline. The wooded bluff rises a thousand feet out of the water, in a slope too steep for roads or houses. Below the water's surface, the bluff falls in a sharp slant, straight down to depths of forty and fifty fathoms. Some boatmen find this face of Orcas forbidding, but dedicated sport fishermen relentlessly probe these deeps, all year around, idling along the bluff looking deceptively indolent. More often than not, they are rewarded for their efforts.

Cruise Four temporarily abandons Orcas Island at Point Lawrence, not because the shoreline looks ominous, but because we want to reach Clark Island and encircle Lummi.

It is not easy to judge the length of time it will take to reach Clark on this cruise. If you explore a number of small coves on Orcas along the way, you might average eight knots on power for the run, arriving off Clark by midmorning. If you are a bit slower, Clark makes a good lunch stop. In either case, since you may choose to spend the night here after circling Lummi Island, this is a good time to look around and check out the amenities.

Clark Island State Marine Park is a long, narrow rib of rock that rises twenty to thirty feet out of the water for most of its length. You can hike the crest of this rib; it makes a short but delightful walk. The island is less than a mile long.

At its southern tip Clark broadens slightly, just enough to form a comfortable hook around a little cove on the island's east side. Here you will find half a dozen mooring buoys, a beach of gray shingle and sand, sunny hollows filled with flowering shrubs, and thickets of alder and maple trees. Sheltering this pocket is a dense framework of black green firs. Two small parks-department signs, some picnic tables, trash containers, well-shrouded pit toilets, and several slim paths are all the improvements you will find on this unspoiled sliver of an island. The hand of man has touched it but lightly, then passed on.

And so should you. It would be well to leave Clark by noon or soon after. *Should* is an unpleasant word on a vacation cruise—let's amend it. Our estimates of hours do not really matter unless you are on a limited schedule and must keep to the timetable we have proposed for Cruise Four. According to our plan, you will spend this first night either at Clark Island or at a spot farther along. That means you will need to cruise around Lummi Island and return to Clark in the afternoon; at eight knots it should take you just over two hours to make this loop. *However,* does anyone cruise without slowing to enjoy beautiful spots, or dropping anchor for lunch, or pursuing something that is not quite clear in the binoculars: duck or eagle, swan or seal, or a curious mat of seaweeds? Your time is your own. Just keep in mind that it is at least seventeen miles around Lummi from Clark—more if you hug the Lummi shore.

Promising yourselves a longer exploration of the isolated little park on Clark Island, you now head east across Rosario Strait, making for the light at Village Point. The crossing here is about two miles, and what chop there is in midchannel will not jostle you for long. The Vessel Traffic Lanes run across your course, leading freighters and other deep-draft vessels north to Cherry Point or to the Canadian Traffic Lanes that feed big commercial vessels into the Port of Vancouver. Tugs pass, pulling barges of sawdust for paper mills; purse seiners and gill-netters and small coastal cargo vessels hurry up and down Rosario Strait, cutting sharp wakes; the water surface looks like hammered metal and breaks the sun's reflection into thousands of flashing triangles. Crossing, you will look north and south along one of the region's two major water highways between the United States and Canada. Where it broadens, north of Lummi Island, the wide expanse of Georgia Strait begins.

If you are unfamiliar with the Puget Sound Vessel Traffic System, it will be worth your while to note the ways that the system affects pleasure craft operation. The VTS was introduced in 1972 as a safety measure for averting collisions between vessels. Water routes that are the most heavily used by large ships have been divided into traffic lanes, and the flow of traffic in these lanes is constantly monitored by a Coast Guard station in Seattle. The lanes are clearly marked on NOAA charts of the region and, in the waters themselves, by vertically striped, midchannel buoys. The small-craft skipper is obliged to observe these lanes by moving with the flow of traffic rather than against it. If he crosses the lanes, he is required to do so at a right angle and when the lanes are clear of large vessels. In no case should he cross the bow of a large vessel with less than a half-mile clearance, nor should he come closer abeam or astern of a large craft than 500 yards.

Lummi Island offers a remarkable profile from any direction. Long and narrow, like a much-magnified Clark Island, it lies like a barricade off the entrance to Bellingham Bay. Its south half is a sharp-backed mountain, almost two thousand feet tall, that ends as a wicked-looking rock reef at Carter Point. The great face of this uplift looks toward the mainland and is coated thickly with Douglas fir, spruce, cedar, and pine. Rising rapidly from the water's edge, it shelters a line of shallow coves and bights—several of which offer good anchorage, in case you ever need a night's stop in this neighborhood. The other side of the island, however—the face you see as you cross from Clark—looks as if a huge knife had sliced downward, carving out Lummi Peak as a sculptor might break open a block of marble. The slope is too sheer to support a forest. Trees struggle to survive here, and few succeed. From the peak to the waterline, vertical streaks mark the runoff pattern of rainwater; rich patches of brown and red soil over sweeps of purplish rock alternate with the sparse brushy cover that clings to Lummi Island's steepest side.

The long, bumpy ridge that crests this mountain is a landmark in the San Juans. As you discovered on Cruises One and Two, the outline of Lummi lies at the end of many channels, rises misty and gray above nearer, smaller shapes, and catches evening sunlight long after the waters are fully shaded. Many skippers steer their vessels by taking bearings on Lummi Peak. On a foggy day, that distinctive lumpy spine rises above the white shroud, as unmistakable as a beacon.

To the north, Lummi drops suddenly and thrusts out a long lowland covered with trees, houses, and people; it is fringed with fishing boats, buoys, and small rocky points of land. Few spots here are tourist oriented. The island, as its name indicates, was long ago a principal center for the Lummi Indian tribe. Today the reservation itself is on the long mainland peninsula that is separated from the island by Hale Passage, and few Lummis are to be found on the island that bears their tribal name.

Nevertheless, the village at Village Point is a center and anchorage for the kind of fishing boats that the Indians developed: reef-netters. Reef netting is an unusual kind of fishing in which the boats remain anchored and let the fish come to them. Hauled out much of the year, like those you may have noticed on Lopez Island, the boats are reset each June and stay anchored in position, sometimes until late autumn.

Special areas are designated by the state for reef-netting operations. The Lopez Island group fish outside Fisherman Bay, south of the bay's entrance. A substantial set is fixed in position off Shaw Island southeast of Indian Cove, and occasionally a few such boats fish off Stuart Island. But the largest group is here at Village Point.

In a designated area, such as this, the reef-netters line up in rows, linking themselves in pairs. The men in each pair of boats work together, with nets strung between them in the water. A pair of boats is called a "gear," and a fisherman who hopes to earn a living this way will probably own three or four gears. However, many reef-netters (including teachers who have summers free) use this procedure merely to supplement some other income. It is interesting that the Lummis themselves no longer use reef-netters, preferring gill-netters or seiners.

If you do not set out on this cruise too early in the year (before June, that is), your course will take you close to the lines of anchored boats, and you will be able to see the light framework built up inside and above each open hull. This framework enables a sharp-eyed fisherman to climb some eight feet above his boat, like a sailor in rigging. From a platform at that level he is strategically positioned to peer down into the water's depths and sight schools of fish. It looks like a precarious perch, so you will understand the purpose of the pole rising above it or the railing that sometimes guards it.

From Village Point (where there is a good marina) to Point Migley, Lummi is lined with a scattering of houses, most of them recently built. Farms lie behind and above them on the gently rolling lowlands, and you can see cattle pastured on green slopes or ambling along a fence line.

Give Point Migley plenty of room as you round the tip of the island into Hale Passage. The reef that extends from it is hazardous, even though skippers who know the area tend to fish right on top of it.

Hale Passage (or "Hale's Pass," as we most often hear it called) is a beautiful stretch of water. For close to an hour you can run parallel to Lummi and enjoy a constantly changing vista. Shaping the passage to port will be the blunt end of Lummi Peninsula where Fishermans Cove Marina occupies Gooseberry Point and the Lummi Island ferry takes island residents home after a day's work in Bellingham or Ferndale.

The marina has a float that will hold four boats, an overhead marine way, a well-stocked grocery store, fuel, water, marine parts, and a repair service. There is also a coffee shop and a restaurant, which is the favorite gathering place for residents of the peninsula and for sport fishermen who keep their boats in the marina's extensive dry-storage facility.

Beyond the marina is the northeastern shore of Hale's Pass, which features some beautiful beaches, a small-craft launching facility maintained by Whatcom County, and a bluff. If you arrive around the twentieth of June, you may happen upon the annual Lummi Indian Stommish, which features races between the great war canoes of tribes from up and down the whole inland sea.

At low tide the peninsula shore beyond the bluff stretches into a ribbon of sand—a shalelike, beveled ridge that ties the mainland to little Portage Island. This ribbon of sand, broad and solid enough to support a car, is the Portage, and it disappears under each rising tide. The three Jones brothers, who own and operate Fishermans Cove Marina, warn all who will listen about the Portage. They know the temptation it poses. From Hale Passage, the city of Bellingham (at the upper end of Bellingham Bay) is handsomely framed by Lummi Peninsula and Portage Island. At high or half tide you feel sure you can turn between them and head for the appealing city that spreads itself like a Riviera town over the hills across the bay. But you cannot. Every once in a while someone tries it and rips out the keel of his boat. When visible and dry, the Portage belongs to the Lummi Indian tribe. No one but tribal members may cross it without permission.

You will run southeastward along Hale Passage, in the lee of Lummi Island. Beautiful, tempting little coves dot the island shoreline. Much traffic from Bellingham will join you as you approach the narrow water between Eliza Island and Carter Point, some of it heading for the small anchorages that indent Lummi: Inati Bay (the shores of which are private property), Reil Harbor, or one of the new-moon slivers of log-crested sand that will shelter about one boat each.

Eliza Island, to port, was named for the Spanish explorer Francisco Eliza, whose 1791 expedition sent sailing vessels of substantial draft into—among other places—the shallows of Bellingham Bay. The island is small and graceful and owned by far-sighted Northwesterners who have built vacation homes along its sheltered shores. It has no public access, but its outlines enhance our cruise, and its small coves provide excellent temporary anchorage.

Rounding Carter Point and heading northwestward, you will see again the cluster of almost motionless vessels that marks good fishing grounds. Here, too, divers find the rock-channeled deeps full of good things, including starfish, abalone, and that long, brownish, slimy marine curiosity, the sea cucumber.

Now Lummi Peak rises above you and your course lies near the knife-sharp slope that supports it. Close to the sparsely covered cliff, you can see that some of its striations were caused by rock slides, so you may move slightly farther offshore. It is in this area that our boat was once paced by a playful school of dolphins, who arched and plunged alongside of us for perhaps half a mile. Beyond Lummi Rocks, which you can pass either to port or starboard, a northwesterly course will bring you back for the night to Clark Island.

If the mooring buoys inside the hook on Clark Island are taken, you can anchor nearby or go around to the west side of the island where there are three more mooring buoys. The latter position is more sheltered from the wash of heavy traffic on Rosario Strait, so for us it is sometimes a first choice.

As the day draws to a close you may want to walk the rocks around the south end of Clark and watch the flocks of gulls settle into their multilevel apartments on The Sisters. Or perhaps you will explore the tide pools along the shore.

Alternate moorage to consider if Clark is crowded is in the Sucia Islands (which we will explore in Cruise Five), a short run to the northwest, or—if you need supplies, fuel, or a restaurant meal ashore—Bartel's Marine Resort, on the north shore of Orcas. Bartel's is the first destination of the second day, so staying there puts you a little ahead on Cruise Four.

A morning run along the cliff shore of Orcas starts your day if you stayed at Clark. The sun is behind you, the big island looms grandly ahead, and salmon may leap from the waters off your bow. This is one of the region's finest salmon fishing spots.

Bartel's marina is located on Terrill Beach just east of where Mount Constitution drops to a saddle of low land between East Sound and President Channel. In fact, it looks on the chart as if the sea is trying to cut Orcas Island in two at this point. Little more than a mile away across the saddle from Bartel's lie Ship Bay and Fishing Bay at the head of East Sound, and covering much of that saddle is the village of Eastsound. You can tie up at Bartel's dock or buoys and hike into town. It is a substantial walk along a tree-lined road, and the shops of Eastsound offer varied goods in surroundings of much charm. A fine old inn facing south down East Sound supplies excellent meals in a nineteenth-century atmosphere, and the view down the fjord is magnificent.

The *Islands' Sounder,* a weekly newspaper, issues from this community. Pick up a copy; reading it gives you an immediate feeling for island living. You cannot really empathize with islanders by merely coasting along island shores.

The village also leads to Moran State Park, which spreads over the summit of Mount Constitution. This land, which provides vacation joy for thousands every year, was only one of the gifts Robert Moran showered on early residents of Orcas Island.

Is this your moment to climb the mountain that you have now almost circled? Probably not, unless you can arrange to get to its south face by car (taxi?). The only access road to the mountain goes up that side. So for now we will leave the eastern wing of Orcas Island and head west.

You may wonder at the infrequent breaks in the shoreline, the few docks and floats, the great stretches of undeveloped wooded shore and hillside running down President Channel to Steep Point. However, a glance at the chart should provide explanations. Orcas Island is oriented southward. Its roads terminate at the town of Orcas on the southern edge of its central mass, because it is here that the state ferry docks, bringing residents and visitors, supplies and mail. Here it takes on passengers and vehicles and commodities bound for the mainland. This is the economic heart of the island. The primary road runs north, then east to Eastsound and almost to Point Lawrence, but westward its main branch stays near the inner waters of West Sound and Deer Harbor. On the northern shore you are far away from the center of island life.

You see only nature's show for some ten miles after clearing Parker Reef, as you remain near the Orcas Island shoreline and follow it down to Spring Passage. Above you now is the second noteworthy uplift of this generally massive island. From far away, Orcas Knob is a distinctive shape, easily identified by mariners who are either lost or befogged. It stands close to the shore, rising dome-shaped from sea level to 1,050 feet. Behind it the ground rises again in the broadened Turtle Back Range, which climbs another five hundred feet into the air. As you pass below these great forested hills, you will have Waldron Island to starboard. Although much of Waldron is low-lying, even sandy, the face it shows you as you run down President Channel is its highest, as though it needed to come up with some answer to the challenge of Orcas Knob.

On Cruise Two you made the acquaintance of Jones Island. It is hard to suppose that you will be able to pass it casually now, ignoring its siren call. You may decide to angle over into the northern bay of Jones Island for a repeat visit, just to see if your memory has exaggerated its charms. But first decide where you would like to spend the second night of Cruise Four. If you stayed at Bartel's and enjoyed Eastsound, you may not have left that part of the island until lunchtime or after. In that case, the day is now dwindling and you will want to find a night's moorage soon. In Deer Harbor, just around Steep Point, you will find good possibilities. It is sensible to reduce speed going through North Pass into Deer Harbor, by the way. We have never entered the inner waters through this opening without encountering much drift: deadheads, mostly, and considerable seaweed. Once you are inside, Deer Harbor spreads a handsome panorama before you. Alone in the water, little Fawn Island adds to the attractions of this triangular inlet.

You will by now begin to think that deer form a kind of motif on and around Orcas Island. There was Deer Point at Obstruction Pass; then Doe Island and Doe Bay. There is a tiny community of Doebay above Doe Bay, and Buck Mountain is one of the outriders beneath Mount Constitution. The village of Olga, you may have noticed, is located on a small indentation called Buck Bay. Now you are near Fawn Island in Deer Harbor. The names are everywhere, and for a reason. In the days when only Indians visited these islands, deer abounded on Orcas. The Lummis venerated one spot on the eastern shore of East Sound where, according to tradition, the first deer was created. In 1852 some of the first Caucasians to settle on Orcas arrived by canoe in Deer Harbor and set up a hunting camp. Their purpose was to supply venison to the relatively populous community at Victoria on Vancouver Island. For years they "farmed" deer, shipping out the precious flesh in large canoes.

On at least one occasion, these settlers reversed the process and transported five live cows from Victoria to Deer Harbor by canoe! And one wonders: How? Were the creatures standing up, peering with stretched necks over the side? Surely not. On their sides, then, feet tied; huge, liquid brown eyes rolling in panic; bellowing, singly or in concert? No? Then how did they do it? How would you yourself, paddling a canoe, transport a live cow over some twenty miles of water? Well, one has always known the pioneers were hardy stock.

Today, incidentally, deer still roam widely over Orcas. If you drive on the island, early in the morning or after dark, you will see them briefly before they dart among the trees and are out of sight. Headlights will reflect from their startled eyes.

In your boat, taking Fawn Island to port, you now head up Deer Harbor to a scene of much activity. This is Deer Harbor Marina, and it makes a good night's stop—if they have room for you. The inn on the hill above the marina is famous for its chicken dinners. Gas, ice, showers, cabins, heated indoor swimming pool, post office, laundry, small grocery, restaurant, pub—all these amenities are available at Deer Harbor. A branch of the primary island road runs through the resort (do not worry; it is not a highway, just a narrow macadam road), so

Broken Point on Shaw Island, at the end of Harney Channel

you can walk up to the head of the harbor and cross to the other side, where the marine views will have you exclaiming and taking photos and longing for a sketchbook.

The last day of Cruise Four takes you through Pole Pass, across the mouth of or into West Sound, past Broken Point, and through the singularly handsome passage that is called Harney Channel. If you reached Deer Harbor too early on the second day to want to stop, you may already have run through these waters and moored for the night at Blind Island, across the channel in Blind Bay on Shaw Island. But we will assume that you begin the morning by shooting the narrows at Pole Pass.

This opening between Crane and Orcas islands looks narrower than it is; ferries have been known to navigate it. However, as you approach you notice a rapid current running through the passage, and the shores on both sides look as if they could present problems.

Shallows and mats of seaweed crowd you into a midchannel course, and that is exactly where you should go—as close to the center as possible.

You may encounter other vessels coming or going ahead of you, idling for their own turns at the pass, or circling while a series of boats shoots through from the other side. The water is often chopped in many directions, and if your vessel is small, you may have a bumpy transit. But Pole Pass is a must. Beyond it you can look down a shining avenue with openings to port and to starboard. Small craft—sail, power, open, and decked—dot the water. You are seeing all the way to Blakely Island, on the far side of East Sound. This is Harney Channel, named for General William S. Harney, who was one of the more aggressive and excitable officers commanding American forces in the Pig War (see Cruise Two). Like Pickett, he was almost eager to fire on the opposition. Thinking a little further than he, Harney's superiors kept him in check, but his name remains in the islands, reminding us of the brinkmanship of an earlier day.

If you have time, a run up West Sound is rewarding. With the exception of Haida Point, the shores above it are low-lying, undulating hills. The names Haida Point, Massacre Bay, Skull Island, and Victim Island reflect a time when the generally peaceful Lummi Indians, living an almost nomadic life among the San Juans, were subjected to frequent attacks by the warlike northern tribes, the Haidas particularly. Encampments and clam feasts were rarely secure against these raiders who killed or captured their victims, impressing into slavery those whom they took away with them.

The little community of West Sound is located near Haida Point and consists of a small grocery store, a gas pump for cars, a post office, the Orcas Island Yacht Club, and West Sound Bay Marina. Most of the services you might need are available at the marina, and the little yacht club makes an engaging shape on the shoreline, looking like a diminutive frame house with a peaked roof. Temporary moorage is permitted at the pier in front of the club, allowing you enough time to enjoy the beautiful walk along the road to the marina. You cross a small bridge topping a stream that cascades in miniature falls and rills over tumbled rocks. A small pond attracts seabirds, and overhead you might spot the brilliant flash of a western tanager on the wing. Or a bald eagle.

The town of Orcas on Harney Channel sits high on a bluff. Arriving or leaving by ferry, visitors must negotiate a sharp incline, and the row of cars awaiting the ferry's arrival strings up the hillside like a decoration. A cluster of buildings and fuel storage tanks clings to the cliff face without apparent support, so that you half expect the whole community to tumble out into the water. Beneath the town is an old

West Sound on Orcas Island

and rather fragile wharf, where the wash from many passing vessels (including ferries) makes moorage precarious.

About a quarter of a mile farther to the east, a jetty and the always attractive massing of masts mark a small marina. Between the wharf and the jetty is the ferry landing. Since you are now in waters where one or another of the ferries serving the islands is almost always in sight, you might like to know something of this service.

Frequently under attack today for its economic shortcomings, the state ferry line that serves the islands dates back to the 1920s when Captain Harry W. Crosby organized the first ferry run through the islands as an experiment. Captain Crosby's vessel, *Harvester King,* was almost one hundred feet long and could carry a dozen cars. Before it came to the islands, the only means of transportation were smaller sail- and then steam-powered boats, which could carry nothing more than people and goods. Automobiles were proliferating by then, and Crosby saw a need for vessels that could carry them. He established ferry terminals at Anacortes on Fidalgo and Sidney on Vancouver, where the ferry runs begin and end today.

The success of Crosby's experiment is before your eyes: huge, state-owned, green and white, multideck vessels running every hour in summer, serving Orcas, Shaw, Lopez, and San Juan islands. Not all ferries complete the trip to Sidney, since traffic does not warrant it, but those who make the ferry excursion round trip from Anacortes to Sidney will have a magnificent experience.

The town of Orcas is pleasant to explore, and here, too, you can enjoy some delightful walks along the island's roads, particularly the one that runs along a bluff overlooking the water.

Across Harney Channel from Orcas is the Shaw Island ferry landing, and offshore, looking totally unimportant and useless, is little Blind Island. But look again. The small mound, sparsely covered with short grasses and shrubs and old stunted trees, may remind you of a balding head, but its rocky, broken shoreline has deep fissures and miniature promontories. Clear waters swirl around it, washed up by passing vessels, and behind Blind Island, like a great canopy, is Blind Bay. Do stop at this island, if only briefly. There are three convenient mooring buoys behind Blind Island, and the island itself is a state marine park, less well known than most. Circle east of the island to avoid rocks and reefs that make dangerous the deceptively open-looking western passage between it and Shaw.

Because hasty cruising parties do not seem attracted to this spot, the buoys of the Blind Island park are likely to be empty. But you have come to dinghy heaven. Lower the little boat and set out around Blind Island. Soon you will be dawdling from one small inlet to another. Starfish and sea anemones and fingerlings are visible through the clear water. Broad-leaved seaweeds make an underwater garden. You can clamber ashore at many spots and scour the rocks and grasses for small creatures. Butterflies like Blind Island. So do birds. Wild flowers bloom among the grasses. Presently, you will tie your dinghy to a rock or log or pull it up on a tiny beach, and you will conquer the heights, all twenty or thirty feet of them. It is a miniature world, and it induces slowness, sleepy breathing, and relaxed scannings of the varied horizons. The air is exquisitely clean, and a light breeze almost always blows in from Harney Channel. On Blind Bay you will doubtless see several sailboats—not racing sailboats, but small, indolent vessels, curving and sweeping their white triangles against the secretive jade and blue black waters—waters washing shores that are dotted with quiet houses and spread with golden green meadows. Fantasy. It is a place for dreams.

And now Cruise Four is almost completed. Leaving Blind Bay you will pass through the narrowest part of Harney Channel, where reaching headlands from Shaw and Orcas suggest a time when the two islands were linked, a geologic unit. Easy to miss as you pass this narrows is little Grindstone Harbor, a rocky but popular anchorage on the Orcas side. In the days when early settlers were clearing land for small farms, a man named Paul Hubbs settled here, bringing his grindstone with him. It was the only grindstone in the San Juans. Everyone sought out Hubbs in his tiny, rock-obstructed bay, carrying dulled tools that needed sharpening. In a way, Hubbs's story is similar to that of Moran. A heart condition forced him to give up the lively store that he had established on the basis of his grindstone's popularity; when told by his physician that he had only a few months to live, he became an island hopper with no fixed address, eating berries and fish, sleeping on the ground. He lived for thirty-eight more years.

Rounding Foster Point, Shag Rock, and Diamond Point, you will find yourself facing the narrowing neck of East Sound, and there across the open water is the starting point of this voyage, whether it was Rosario Resort, Olga, or the Obstruction Pass Boating Area.

And now that you have seen so much of the islands, been through so many channels, located so many landmarks—now may be the best time to scale Mount Constitution and see what they all look like from above. It is only three miles from Olga to the mountain's top, and good climbers enjoy the hike.

On the summit of Mount Constitution is a stone lookout tower. From this eminence you can see all the islands strewn below, washed by shining channels, dotted with lakes, lightly etched with slim, meandering roads. Forests and meadows, hills and dales, farms and isolated summer cabins decorate the lands, in pleasing balance. The waters far below are flecked with boats, ferries, and navy vessels; tide lines and currents give texture to their surfaces, changing the water's color from glittering cream to sheet metal, from deep reflective blue to forest green.

All the lands and waters from Vancouver Island to the mainland, from the Canadian Coast Range to the Olympics are spread before you. There is no more magnificent view in the entire Northwest.

You may not have time today, but at *some* point in your cruising you should scale Mount Constitution, if only to examine the largest existing chart of where you went on Cruises One, Two, Three, and Four.

Is it time to head for home? The quickest course is through Obstruction or, for variety, Peavine Pass, then south down the Blakely Island shore to the narrowest crossing of Rosario Strait near Strawberry Island. Just south of Cypress Island is Guemes Channel and a familiar approach to Anacortes.

Inner and Outer Islands of the Gulf

Cruises Five through Eight lace in and out among the Gulf Islands of Canada. If you have enough days to spare, we suggest that you join two or more of the cruises together. It will probably take you a long time to reach your starting point at Bedwell Harbour or Nanaimo, and you may as well be able to enjoy a long cruise when you get there. The days required for these cruises, as we have estimated them, *do not include the length of time it takes you to reach each starting point.*

Let's begin with a simple matter of identification—or is it so simple? Just what are the Gulf Islands? Do they all lie north of the San Juans? Is Vancouver Island one of them? What about those islands that lie north of the city of Vancouver and beyond Howe Sound?

The Gulf Islands of Canada are scattered north and south over a substantial range of latitude. When the Spanish explorers found the first of them in 1791, no one could tell for sure that they were all islands. It was thought that perhaps some were attached to what was then considered the "great peninsula." This supposed peninsula was later found to be an island and was named for Captain George Vancouver.

Within a year or two, Spanish and English explorers had discovered most of the channels that we know today. The captains of Spain put names on those waterways and islands that appeared important to them as explorers and navigators: San Juan "Archipiélago," Punta de Saturnina (now known as East Point, on Saturna Island), Galiano, Valdes, Gabriola, and Gran Canal de Nuestra Senora del Rosario la Marinera for the largest body of water leading north—no doubt hoping it was the eagerly sought Northwest

Passage. Even though the Nootka Convention of 1790 between Spain and Britain marked the beginning of Spain's withdrawal from the Northwest, many of the old Spanish names remained.

In 1792 Captain Vancouver charted the Gran Canal and renamed it the Gulf of Georgia in honor of his embattled king, George III. Some sixty-five years later Captain George Richards resurveyed the great inland sea and changed its name to the *Strait* of Georgia in the interest of greater accuracy. But the residents of Vancouver Island, the mainland coast, and the islands between continued to refer to their sea as "the Gulf." And when the international boundary between Canada and the United States was finally drawn down Haro Strait in 1872, the islands on the Canadian side of the line became known as the Gulf Islands. Skippers who visit the region today will find that local residents still refer to the Strait of Georgia as the Gulf. But for clarity we will use the official designation—Strait—in the cruises that follow. When referring to the Gulf Islands we will mean those islands lying off the lee shore of Vancouver Island, north of Satellite Channel, Shute Passage, and Prevost Passage, and south of Departure Bay.

It is true that James and Sidney islands—just across Haro Strait from San Juan—may also be considered Gulf Islands; so may Coal and Brethour, and, far to the north, Texada. But in practice, when a skipper plans a cruise to the Gulf Islands, he is thinking of a fan-shaped set of landfalls, widest along the east-west leg of Haro Strait and narrowing northward to end off the shore from Nanaimo. Outside one edge of the fan is Vancouver Island, which lifts a thick spine of mountains and hills to the west and stops Pacific storms before they can reach the inner islands. To the east of the fan is the wide-open strait, wide enough and long enough to permit buildups of heavy weather. Those islands that face the strait line up like a battalion, lifting one almost continuous ridge from East Point on Saturna to Orlebar Point on Gabriola. They are often referred to as the "outer Gulf Islands."

Interruptions in this ridge—Active Pass, Porlier Pass, Gabriola Passage—form the portals through which Vancouver yachtsmen enter the "inner Gulfs." Protected east and west, the channels that curve around inside the Gulf Islands make some of the most beautiful cruising waters in the world. One thinks of Port Browning, Plumper Sound, Trincomali Channel, Stuart Channel, Sansum Narrows. They are uncrowded and open, with magnificent shores nearby and entrancing vistas at every turn.

You will discover that there is a major difference between these northern Gulf Islands and the San Juan Islands. You may not feel it at first, but awareness grows on you. It is the names that begin to impress you: Satellite, Pender, Prevost, Moresby, Plumper, Trincomali, De Courcy, Stuart, Ganges. All these are names of British ships or ship captains and other officers. They were ships of the line—warships— or they were survey vessels; they were British navy officers and cartographers.

Gradually it is borne in upon you that settlers of the Gulf Islands survived because they were tucked firmly under the wing of the Royal Navy. They felled trees and planted small crops during that period when men first observed that the sun never set on the British Empire. All the far-flung domains that—before World War II—we identified as British possessions (colored pink on schoolroom globes, whether commonwealth states or crown colonies) were then linked to the English government by a vast and powerful fleet of warships, as well as by merchantmen. In addition to providing muscle for distant and otherwise unprotected settlements, these naval vessels carried linguists and clergymen, printing presses and food, survey teams, building materials, and coal.

Wind propelled these ships at the beginning of the nineteenth century, but they moved mostly on steam by its end. During those decades when the Gulf Islands were settled—sparsely—by mixed groups of frontiersmen, vessels of the Royal Navy based at Victoria served as their lifeline and defense.

It was not the same in the San Juans. On Cruise Two we described a critical period in island history, 1859 through 1872, and it was clear from the San Juan Island dispute that Britain at that time was represented by ships (her military occupancy maintained by marines) while the United States ferried in infantry. Lines of supply for settlers of Britain's colony tended to be maintained by ships and often stretched halfway around the globe. In contrast, settlement of Friday Harbor and Orcas depended on supplies brought by boat from twenty-mile-distant mainland communities whose own lines of supply were either overland or from coastal commercial shipping out of San Francisco.

Admiral Baynes of the Royal Navy did not want war over the pig that was shot on San Juan Island because—among other reasons—informal arrangements between Britain and the United States allowed supplies and mail from San Francisco to reach Victoria, as well as U.S. settlements. Except for this tenuous tie, Baynes had the Pacific and Indian oceans, the Cape of Good Hope, and the Atlantic between himself and his government, there being no Panama Canal yet—no Suez Canal either, until 1869. His sources of vital commodities were almost as far away as his government, despite supply bases in Hong Kong and the Sandwich Islands. Overland connections between British Columbia and eastern Canadian ports, utilized mostly by Hudson's Bay Company, were fragile and much affected by winter weather.

Because land routes were unreliable, all settlement in the crown colony at first relied heavily on the Royal Navy. And out of that period of dependence on the specific, physical presence of anxiously awaited individual vessels came most of the names that you will find in the Gulf Islands, even though a few of the original Spanish names were retained. We will identify them for you, while the various cruises lead you along the same water corridors that were patrolled by Queen Victoria's sailors in the mid-nineteenth century, when Canada's frontier spanned the "Gulf" of Georgia.

We begin with Cruise Five.

Cruise
Five

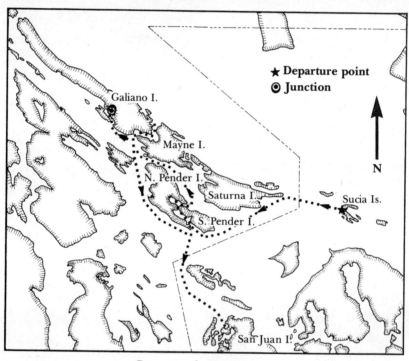

★ Departure point
◉ Junction

Galiano I.

Mayne I.

N. Pender I.

Saturna I.

S. Pender I.

Sucia Is.

N

San Juan I.

Do not use for navigation.
Use NOAA 18423, Folio Small-Craft Chart, and Canadian Hydrographic
Service Small Craft Chart 3310

The Penders and Active Pass

Point of departure: Shallow Bay on the Sucia Islands
Course: via Haro Strait to Bedwell Harbour, Shark Cove, Port Browning, Plumper Sound, Active Pass; return through Active Pass, Trincomali Channel or Swanson Channel and Haro Strait to Roche Harbor
Stops: Bedwell Harbour, Miners Bay, Sturdies Bay, Montague Harbor
Length of cruise: approximately 52 nautical miles to Roche Harbor; 34 nautical miles to junction with Cruise Six
Duration on power: 2 days
Duration on sail: 3 to 6 days
Overnight moorage:
    First night: Sturdies Bay
    Second night: Montague Harbour Marine Park or Roche Harbor
Junction with Cruise Six: Montague Harbour Marine Park

Narrow Channels,
Winding Channels

Shallow Bay is one of the four major havens on the Sucia Islands, which collectively form one of Washington's most popular marine parks. Masses of yachtsmen all up and down Puget Sound are devoted to "Sucia," as the park is commonly known. Located north of Orcas, Sucia, like Damascus, seems to be situated where all roads meet and cross. Whenever we intend to move out west or north of the San Juans, we spend our first night at Sucia. Of the four embayments in the park, Fossil Bay, on the southeastern corner, is the most heavily used. It is well supplied with mooring buoys, has two busy sets of floats, and boasts good, protected anchorage. Ashore there are camping sites, pleasant beaches, wooded trails, picnic tables, fire rings, fresh water, and pit toilets. Echo Bay, on the northeast, is the largest of Sucia's havens and a bit more open to the wind, a fact that makes it a favorite of sailors. Echo Bay has no floats, but there are a few mooring buoys and some secure anchorage. Ashore, trails connect with Fossil Bay and other island points. There are campsites, tables, water, and toilets. Little Fox Cove is across a narrow isthmus from Fossil Bay, on the southwest side. It shares Fossil Bay's shoreside amenities. There are a few mooring buoys, but the cove is a favorite for skippers of day boats, who beach their craft here and set up camp nearby.

Shallow Bay is on the west side, looking out toward the Gulf Islands. Ringed and protected by a high ridge, it offers mooring buoys and a long, sandy beach. This is real sand, the kind that makes sand castles. Thickly forested, the land beyond the beach hides tables, fire rings, pit toilets, and paths that lead to other legs of the spidery islands. Terminating the beach at one end is a bald sandstone cliff with weatherworn, rounded edges that protrude into the bay. The sandstone is topped with grasses and a path that is invisible from the water, but people walking that path make bold silhouettes against the sky. They look ready to pitch out into the sea at any moment. A giant crack cuts open the sandstone face, leaving a kind of flue that is about two feet wide. Convenient boulders, grotesquely eaten by the tides, allow you to reach this crack and, if you are small and agile, to climb it, inching straight upward with back and feet braced.

Aboard the twenty or thirty boats at rest on the surface of the bay, there are always clusters of people—on deck or in cockpits—their eyes continually drawn to the spectacle of children climbing the sandstone flue or hikers standing on the precarious ledge above.

The floor of Shallow Bay catches and holds anchors admirably, but it *is* shallow. Check the tide tables, and anchor well out toward the middle or take a mooring buoy. If you put the hook down close to shore, you may find yourselves beached during the night, as we once did.

In the morning it is time to set out for Active Pass by way of Bedwell Harbour. It would be closer to head directly for Active Pass, but you need to clear Canadian customs at Bedwell before you can start your exploration.

The mouth of Shallow Bay, as you undoubtedly discovered when you arrived, looks quite broad, but it is constricted by a ragged stone reef on the north side and a resident mat of seaweed on the south side. Passing between the two beacons that mark these hazards, you take off across a wide stretch of Haro Strait. Strangely enough, unlike the often turbulent southern stretches of Haro, this wide area where the strait pours into Boundary Pass and President Channel is often quiet. Surfaces like sheet metal may lie between you and the shore of Saturna Island. A westerly course will serve you well for this crossing. It will line you up between East Point on Saturna and Mount Constitution on Orcas. Little Skipjack Island will be abeam to port, and Patos Island will be off the starboard aft quarter.

Boundary Pass is a traffic lane for ocean-going vessels, mostly cargo ships. We watch for them rather carefully, because they move at a faster speed and small craft can be much inconvenienced by their bow waves and wakes. Like trains, they cannot slow or stop quickly, so it is up to us to keep out of their way.

You will want to close up on Saturna Island until you are offshore a comfortable distance for cruising—perhaps a hundred yards, if you are like us. Then, changing course, you will run beside Saturna and South Pender until you reach Bedwell Harbour. In the process you will cross the mouth of Narvaez Bay, named for the captain of the first Spanish vessel in these waters, and Plumper Sound, a broad avenue separating the two mountainous islands. This is a beautiful run; you have only to maintain your heading and enjoy it. Since you cannot go ashore until you have cleared customs, you must wait until later to explore the shoreline.

East Point is bare. A cluster of small white buildings with red roofs constitute the important lighthouse installation that occupies it, and a light tower next to the house is also painted red. The ground rises sharply behind East Point, and sheer cliffs fall to the water all the way to Narvaez Bay. Monarch Head, on the far side of Narvaez Bay, is high and rocky, topped with firs wherever the trees have found a grip. On a northwest line, the steep mass of the island lifts above the shoreline for some three unbroken miles. This uplift is called Brown Ridge and you see it marching away at an angle up Plumper Sound. Mount Warburton Pike—1,630 feet tall—is its highest point and makes a good mariner's landmark.

In the water near you, Java Islets are merely the tips of a long narrow reef that parallels the Saturna shoreline beyond Monarch Head. We recommend you stay well out from them and head across Plumper Sound for Blunden Islet. Although it will seem to you that little Blunden lies right in the mouth of Plumper Sound, it is actually a tip of peninsula broken off from Teece Point on South Pender. Almost bare, revealing deeply striated stone, Blunden Islet sports a fringe of firs that rises like a thin crest from its north side, a good indication of the direction and force of winter winds in this area. Beyond it you can glimpse lots of small-boat traffic, sail and power, crossing Plumper Sound farther to the north.

Higgs Point, Gowlland Point, and Tilly Point overlap ahead of you, hiding the entrance to Bedwell Harbour. Wooded and marked with occasional small homes, this shoreline has a curious tranquility. Other boats besides yours run along in front of it, but few appear to stop.

The entrance to Bedwell Harbour is immediately obvious as you approach from Tilly Point (in contrast to the approach you make on Cruise Three). Reaching toward you from the port bow are the rocky pincers around Peter Cove, but this time they seem well out of the way, and you again feel that the primary hazard is from small-boat traffic. In and out, by twos and threes, go all kinds of pleasure craft: tiny outboards, big two-masted schooners, floating gin palaces with canopied flying bridges, day boats, catamarans. Overhead you are likely to see one or more seaplanes descending to the busy harbor. And in the distance beyond South Pender Island you can identify the largest, most imposing massif in the Gulf Islands: the southern mountains on Salt Spring.

A light at Hay Point marks the Bedwell Harbour entrance; just beyond are the floats of the Canadian customs station and Bedwell Harbour Marine Resort.

Your customs stop probably will be brief, even if you arrive in high summer. The clearance itself is not complicated, but we have reviewed it for you in "Crossing the Line," as you will remember if you followed Cruise Three. Our own experience prompts us to think that no one engaged in bettering international relations anywhere can do better than the pleasant, smiling officials at Bedwell.

It's lunchtime. If you are content to prepare your own lunch from the galley, you will find it pleasant to eat while berthed at the Bedwell Harbour Resort, which gives you a fine display of boats and planes, all anxiously maneuvering to approach the customs floats in proper order. Safely through the process yourself, you will gleefully note all the mistakes others make—and there are a great many. One fifty-foot powerboat backs cautiously away from the dock only to miss by inches the stern of another, similarly engaged. A small sailboat, anxious to tie up on wind power, narrowly escapes being driven too far inshore where hidden shallows threaten his keel. A small seaplane thunders in, crossing the stern of a circling cruiser, and almost clips the flying bridge with its flying wings. Everyone except those actively engaged in mooring or releasing lines is in high good humor and the air is full of amiable shouts, cheers, and laughter. The most commonplace sandwich tastes like *boeuf bourguignon* under circumstances like these.

The floats of Bedwell Harbour nestle close to a gleaming rock wall, which is broken into natural facets and crevices and is wet with runoff from the hill above. Cut into this rock face is the name "HMS Egeria" and the date "1905." During that year the men of that ship were stationed at Bedwell while making a hydrographic survey. They left this mark when they departed.

Curving to the right is a road that goes inland from the customs wharf. It is the only substantial road on South Pender Island, and it leads you on a wonderful stroll. You first climb the abrupt incline from the waterfront, then walk along the paved road between woods of fir, madrona, juniper, and alder. The verge is a mass of grasses and wild flowers. You glimpse a shimmer of harbor whenever the trees thin out. Meanwhile, birdsong and small woodland creatures claim your attention. Here and there you see a house, perhaps a horse, some cows. The four hundred residents on the Penders tend to congregate on the north island near Port Washington. Smaller South Pender is an isolated preserve, only four and a half miles long. The cars you meet undoubtedly will have come by ferry to Otter Bay, near Port Washington; their drivers will have explored this far because of the seductive scenery along the road.

There are alternatives to lunch in your cockpit, by the way. A meal ashore is available in the pub/lounge at the head of the dock. Before fire destroyed it, a superb restaurant and inn occupied the rise above the small grocery store, and yachtsmen kept it packed on summer weekends. Undaunted by the temporary loss of this facility, they now congregate in the small pub, which proffers a limited menu. Here you can enjoy a panoramic, up-harbor view as well as watch boats maneuver at the customs station.

A third lunch spot is visible across the shallow bight north of the customs and resort buildings; there, at Beaumont Marine Park, you can tie to a mooring buoy, dinghy ashore, and eat your sandwiches on a wide, smiling beach. This is picnic country. A double line of buoys accommodates eighteen boats, and you will be tempted to stay far too long in this idyllic retreat. From the park's promontories, we have seen otters ducking and bobbing among the seaweed bulbs, rolling and diving like children. Trees in the park are dense and sweet smelling. Big smooth madrona limbs reach and stretch in angular patterns, their thin, red bark peeling back from the shining quick wood. There are outflung fingers of rock to explore, a long, sandy beach to comb, and forest paths to walk: we once startled a pygmy owl at breakfast along one of these paths. Low, grassy headlands reached by only slightly "improved" paths make the best picnic grounds.

Ready to move on? The next leg of Cruise Five should offer you quite a surprise, but if you are cruising in a sailboat with fixed keel or tall mast, you will have to forego it. Such sailors must go back the way they came, to Plumper Sound, because ahead the way is shallow, narrow, and bridge-obstructed. The rest of us are going by way of the narrows to Shark Cove. This slender passage near the head of Bedwell Harbour is man-made and rock strewn. It calls for cautious navigation, but all effort is repaid manyfold by the beauty along the way.

The Penders are two islands that used to be one. Looking on a small map like jigsaw puzzle pieces not properly fitted together, they are linked by a bridge over a mere ribbon of water that connects Bedwell Harbour to Port Browning. Passage up this canal is breathtaking, both because of its scenery and its hazards. Boats must go at dead slow speed and in a single line. Small power cruisers easily slip through; sailboats have trouble not only with the depth (one fathom) but with the bridge itself. Vertical clearance is only twenty-six feet. A forty-foot horizontal clearance separates the support pillars of the bridge, but it looks more like ten feet as you cautiously approach. The canal is like a miniature river, with banks beautifully ornamented by rocks and mosses, foot-long sandbars, and overhanging limbs of trees. Even as you focus on the obvious hazards, your mind absorbs the loveliness on all sides.

Fortunately, the narrowest part of this passage is quite short. Beyond lies Shark Cove, a jewelled lagoon bordered on one side by the sand beach of Mortimer Spit park. You pass out of Shark Cove, by this time inured to narrow passages, and find yourself in Port Browning.

Unless you plan a more protracted excursion than Cruise Five was designed to be, you will not spend much time today in Port Brown-

Shark Cove and Pender Canal

ing. Perhaps you can spare half an hour for a quick dip or a wade along the sands of Mortimer Spit, if your vessel is small enough to beach. On another occasion you might come back and explore this slender finger of water that reaches in from Plumper Sound to divide North from South Pender. Over the years the marina located near the head of Port Browning has had many ups and downs. Its location is magnificent, however, and when one owner has found himself forced to suspend operations, another very quickly has taken over. Once well known as Scot's Lair, then as the Puerto Lindo Marina, it is now called Port Browning Marina. It has a thousand feet of dock space and many amenities for visitors, including a snack bar and pub. From a small promontory above it, you can see the whole inlet—a sweep of serene, glittering waters edged by the shadows and reflections of the mountains that line Port Browning. From here Mount Norman is the most prominent feature of South Pender's bumpy spine, a symmetrical cone you will now have seen from several angles.

As you leave the Penders by way of Plumper Sound, it seems appropriate to reflect that Daniel Pender was captain of the H.M.S. *Plumper,* a survey vessel charged with locating and charting the various routes between Victoria and Semiahmoo Bay on the mainland.

You enter Plumper Sound by rounding a particularly vicious-looking reef whose name will probably seem apt: Razor Point. The sound is a wide basin of water edged by a long stretch of North Pender Island and the broken waterlines between Saturna and Mayne islands. Skippers with local knowledge penetrate these waters in to

Curlew Island and on past the Belle Chain Islets to the strait. But most visitors accept local advice and content themselves with exploring inside Plumper Sound. There are mooring floats in Lyall Harbour and in Irish Bay, which is shaped like a large bite out of the side of little Samuel Island.

Many boats traverse Plumper Sound, even though few of them appear to use it as a home port. It is a natural doorway to Haro Strait, if you are moving southward, or to the broad north-south artery of Trincomali Channel, if you want to hurry directly north to Nanaimo. Boat-watching is a great pastime here.

A series of hills lines the straight stretch of Mayne Island that leads you to Dinner Point, where you emerge from Plumper Sound through the wide corridor of Navy Channel. Beyond Dinner Point you will be able to see the entrance to Active Pass, busiest of the Gulf Islands' many passages.

Several kinds of traffic flow through Active Pass. On the water's surface are ferries and private yachts, plying the shortest distance between Vancouver and Victoria. Overhead a few small airplanes parallel this directional flow, with the constant escort of seabirds. In the water beneath, salmon have come in from the sea and are taking the most direct route (through Haro Strait, Swanson Channel, Active Pass, and the Strait of Georgia) to spawning grounds in the Fraser River. Also passing through are cod, halibut, sole, and snapper. If all this traffic kept moving along, there would be no problem, but it does not. The primary troublemakers are the sport fishermen who propose to intercept the fish at this bountiful confluence of waters. Trolling, they idle at the entrance or over the surface of Active Pass, crossing bow and stern among the through traffic. Sometimes they seriously inconvenience the heavy ferries that have no room for extra maneuvering in this curved channel between Mayne and Galiano islands. By law the ferries have the right-of-way, because they cannot be stopped and started up like buses at an intersection. But many skippers of small craft seem unaware of this special provision, and the Royal Canadian Mounted Police patrol boats are frequently called into action to clear idling vessels out of the ferries' paths.

You will want to start looking for ferryboats as you round the light at the end of Enterprise Reef and approach Active Pass. You may see as many as four at one time, converging on Georgeson Bay or the landing in Village Bay, or making off to port down Swanson Channel. Sailors should know that tidal currents in the pass may reach six or seven knots at flood and do cause occasional whirlpools and severe rips. Considering these conditions and all the traffic, we recommend that sailboats negotiate Active Pass at slack water.

And when you are ready to go through, watch for the birds.

Mayne Inn on Mayne Island

Seven bald eagle aeries have been reported in treetops along the pass, and as many as forty eagles have been sighted at one time. Ospreys may also be seen in branches overhanging the water, awaiting a chance to plunge after unwary surfacing fish.

Village Bay, to starboard as you approach the entrance to Active Pass, is the only access by car to Mayne Island; like Sturdies Bay at the northeastern end of this busy waterway, it has a ferry landing. This landing lies outside the narrowest length of the pass itself. Since there is not much to do on foot in Village Bay, a stop here lacks appeal. Instead, making sure that the tide is neither at flood nor at ebb, you will head for Collinson and Helen points, which stand like doorjambs at either side of the pass's entrance. Channel markers to port and starboard indicate that this is a fairly wide doorway, as it needs to be to accommodate deep-draft vessels and British Columbia ferries. Beyond, Georgeson Bay cuts into the side of Galiano Island until it reaches a massive stone bluff; then the water pours southwestward in a wide sweep. Here you can leave the traffic channel and pull aside to the public wharf at Miners Bay on Mayne Island, where there is a fuel dock and a grocery store nearby.

A public or government wharf in Canada is always marked by bright red railings, so you can distinguish them from private or commercially operated marinas. The wharf at Miners Bay is broad and solid. Guest moorage bounces a little in the wash of traffic, but the location is lovely. As you look around, you may begin to feel that the Gulf Islands, in general, bulk higher than the San Juans and have more massive uplifts. Visible from many parts of the archipelago, the great southern mass of Salt Spring Island rises over two thousand feet in several places and sometimes descends in spectacular plunges to sea level. The twin peaks of Sutil Mountain and Mount Galiano on Galiano Island rise nearer to your present position in Miners Bay but are somewhat obscured by closer bluffs. All around, it seems, the land is high, displaying almost no lowlands. Furthermore, these islands have had fewer residents to impose a tamed landscape. The ridges are harsh and trees on their crests are battered by winds. You walk only a short distance from the dock before a thick forest lines the road. The densest nearby population is on the boats that are easing through Active Pass.

Back aboard your own vessel, you will move out into the main Active Pass channel, keeping in mind the often swirling and twisting currents that rush through this passage. Be prepared to increase your speed if it becomes necessary to pull away from back eddies that push you toward the shores.

Beyond Burrill Point on the Galiano side is the shallow but attractive inlet called Sturdies Bay. We recommend that you spend the night here. There are many beautiful sights to see, all within a short walking distance. If you feel like a night ashore, Galiano Lodge is located right on the bank of Sturdies Bay above a short shale beach. The lodge has floats and plenty for vacationers to do: golf, tennis, swimming, and bike rentals; gourmet dining and an attractive little pub. You can rent rooms or comfortable, motellike cabins, well fitted out. The usual

Sandstone boulders at Sturdies Bay

services—laundry, showers, a nearby grocery store, boat fuel—are available.

One of the attractions of Sturdies Bay is the small waterfront, characterized by sandstone boulders that stand taller than a man and are carved by tidal action into strange, exotic shapes. It is hard to resist the temptation to walk among them and to feel the smooth-looking but sandpapery surfaces, the rounded domes and sharp-edged caves. And, after all, why should you resist? A delightful preprandial hour can be passed here, broken probably by the arrival or departure of the ubiquitous ferry.

Prolonged summer daylight in this northern clime makes it possible for you to enjoy rose-tinted twilight excursions. Walk a short distance up the road from the ferry dock and you come to the head of Whaler Bay, in whose sheltered waters are any number of graceful, anchored vessels. Look down on them from the elevated road, and you instantly reach for your camera.

Another road branches to the left, roughly parallel to the pass, and if you are good for a longer walk, you should press on, following the signs to Bellhouse Park. Given to the people of British Columbia by L. T. Bellhouse in 1964, the sweeping parkland is part forest, part open ground. Its approach road is fenced by straight fir and cedar boles, broken here and there by aged arbutus trees. Beyond the forested acreage is a rounded bedrock mass sloping down to Active Pass. The bedrock is covered with a thin layer of soil, capable of supporting little but mosses. Showing here and there through the soil are long, smooth streaks of bedrock, polished by wind and rain. In the forest area a chorus of birdsong, including the call of the varied thrush, sometimes keeps you company. On the bare rock shore mounded above the water you hear a different sound. It is worthwhile to sit down and listen.

At first you sense nothing unusual. Then an insistent murmuring rises above the ordinary outdoor sounds. Presently you locate its source. Past the mouth of Sturdies Bay—especially at flood tide—the waters of Active Pass pour into the Strait of Georgia, producing a water surface that is wrinkled and torn with tide rips. The sound of this turbulence is clearly audible from where you sit. The noise is like an ocean surf, but constant, instead of breaking and receding. In fact, it sounds like water boiling. Overhead the cry of a mew gull is faint against that roar. How was it that you could not hear it at first?

The tidal action in Active Pass is also visible where it sends long, narrow sweeps of choppy water out at angles from both sides of the channel. The most turbulent bit of water is a patch that angles away from the meeting point of both tidal rip lines—the surface here is in excited chop, noticeable even from this distance. It is laced with whitecaps and deep shadows. But a skipper close to water level cannot see this effect and might, in a hapless moment, find himself struggling to get through. It is a very bad patch. You will tuck that information away against a time when you might plan to enter the Strait of Georgia this way. And probably you will think again about the importance of avoiding the pass at flood or ebb.

Another curiosity of Active Pass may present itself as you sit bemused in Bellhouse Park. A throb that is different from the sound of the waters fills the air. A ferry is coming through. Soon great pulsing engines fill the pass with their reverberating rumble, which totally drowns the murmur of tide rips. You watch as the vast hull easily flattens the broken patch of water, tearing it to ribbons with its wake. And now another engine can be identified—this time a small single-wing plane that is flying low through the pass. This poses an interesting puzzle. How high, you wonder, do the wind currents of the passage go? Surely the pilot comes through because of some advantage that the air currents give him; otherwise he would not bother to use the pass when all that open sky suggests a more direct course to anyplace. Now he is almost out of sight. All is silent again, except for the gulls and the boiling water.

Active Pass is, as you see, a fascinating channel. One could spend days here. Weeks. But we will push on and complete Cruise Five.

In the morning you retrace your course through Active Pass (avoiding flood and ebb) without going out into the big strait. Good-bye tide rips. You emerge near Enterprise Reef and make the decision that will determine your return course. If you plan to go on to Cruise Six, now is the time to bear off to starboard, keeping fairly close to the shore of Galiano Island. A gentle curve leads you to Phillimore Point, which marks the small opening into Montague Harbor. Passing eastward through this opening south of tiny Julia Island, you will run down an attractive channel framed by the sharp shoulder of Sutil Mountain and the gentler rise of Parker Island. This course leads you directly to Montague Harbour Marine Park, the departure point for Cruise Six. You have probably arrived in time for lunch, and the park makes an ideal lunch stop. In fact, after the rather long cruising day you spent yesterday, you may be ready to settle into Montague Harbour for the night.

If you wish to return home from Cruise Five, after retracing Active Pass you have several possible routes. One leads around the shore of North Pender to Bedwell Harbour (lunch) and then crosses Haro Strait on a southwesterly heading to take you around Turn Point on Stuart Island. From here you can hug the shore of Stuart before crossing Spieden Channel to Roche Harbor, where you will clear U.S. customs. Or you can head directly across the open water between Turn Point and Roche Harbor. From there a route down San Juan Channel leads south or north around Lopez Island and back to Anacortes once again.

Or you can return to Bedwell through Shark Cove and then go on to Roche Harbor.

Or you can transit Plumper Sound to Haro Strait and cross directly toward San Juan Channel, clearing customs at Friday Harbor.

After clearing customs (see "Crossing the Line"), you can make arrangements for spending the night at Roche or at Friday Harbor. (Don't forget to try the doughnuts at the doughnut shop at Roche!)

Cruise
Six

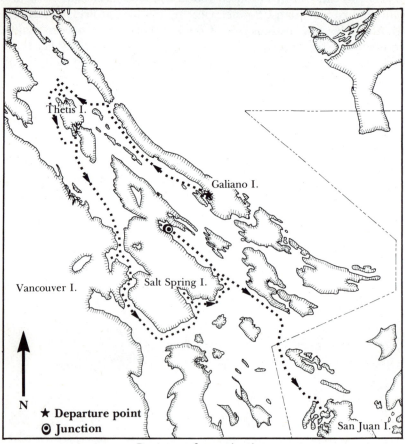

Thetis I.

Galiano I.

Vancouver I.

Salt Spring I.

San Juan I.

N

★ **Departure point**
◉ **Junction**

Do not use for navigation.
Use Canadian Hydrographic Service Small Craft Chart 3310

Trincomali Channel to Ganges by Way of Telegraph Harbour

Point of departure: Montague Harbour Marine Park

Course: via Trincomali Channel, Stuart Channel, Telegraph Harbour, Sansum Narrows, Satellite Channel, Swanson Channel, Ganges Harbour

Stops: Retreat Cove, Telegraph Harbour, Maple Bay, Fulford Harbour

Length of cruise: approximately 62 nautical miles to Ganges, which is the end of Cruise Six and the junction point with Cruise Seven; 83 nautical miles back to Roche Harbor

Duration on power: 2 days

Duration on sail: 3 to 4 days

Overnight moorage:
First night: Telegraph Harbour or Maple Bay
Second night: Ganges Harbour

Junction with Cruise Seven: Ganges, on Salt Spring Island

Broad Channels,
Deep Channels

Montague Harbour has many unexpected charms. We introduced you to this gemlike bay in Cruise Five, as the junction point for those who wished to go directly on to Cruise Six. But now—since you are almost sure to spend one or more nights here—let's look at it more closely.

As you will see from your chart, the harbor is shaped like two bays, one behind the other. Consequently, Montague Harbour, the inside basin, is doubly protected from almost any kind of storm except those blowing in from the northwest. Since the latter are rare in summer, you will probably find Montague somnolently motionless when you arrive. Parker Island, the southwestward barricade, rises only four hundred feet above sea level, but its length and breadth are enough to reduce the force of westerlies. East and south a mountainous terrain, including several prominent peaks, effectively blocks the prevailing southeasterlies of summer.

With depths of two to five fathoms over almost the whole of the bay, Montague Harbour supplies more potential anchorage than yachtsmen need. They are likely to cluster at the north end of the bay where Montague Harbour Marine Park offers a variety of comforts dear to the hearts of boating families. There are thirty-one campsites: some are allocated to boatmen, and some to vacationers in recreational vehicles, a reminder that the park is also accessible by road. Drinking water, trash receptacles, and toilets are provided. Benches are placed where you can sit and overlook the bay, and across the small isthmus to the north, a boat ramp provides launching facilities.

A short wharf stretches out above the beach that rims the park. It is popular for mooring; as a result, its recently lengthened floats, long enough to hold more than a dozen boats, are almost always occupied. We prefer mooring buoys for overnight moorage in any case, and usually we can find a free buoy. We once arrived to find all the buoys had been taken out of the water by the park authorities; so down went the anchor into excellent holding ground. Since then, stronger replacement buoys have been installed, and dot the water like pearls.

Thus far we have said little to explain why Montague Harbour

Montague Harbour on Galiano Island

Marine Park is known as the finest and most popular park in the Gulf Islands. How does one say it? The park's beauty is the kind that you never tire of: unspoiled, natural combinations of water, forest, and hills; brisk, clean air; changing clouds and light patterns; a pervasive feeling of peace.

A great purple bluff of bare stone looms over the bay to the northeast. Scarred horizontally where softer strata have been eaten away, it houses a great many gulls, whose white wings sparkle against the sombre-colored cliff. Beneath this almost vertical wall of stone runs a roadway that connects the park to the small marina, store, fuel dock, and government wharf, which cluster near the ferry landing at the southeast end of the harbor. A walk from the park to the ferry landing and back is just enough exercise to build up your appetite.

The Swartz Bay ferry to the Gulf Islands stops here at Montague Harbour on a regular schedule and brings many visitors, including the campers who share park facilities with yachtsmen. A good paved road runs between this landing and the ferry dock at Sturdies Bay as well as to the campsite area at the park. So here is a point trailerboat skippers may want to remember: boats can be trailered to Galiano Island and launched down the ramp at Montague Harbour Marine Park. Cruise Six could be your first cruise of the summer.

On Galiano, as on all the islands, exploration by foot is profitable. You can hike three miles to the top of Mount Galiano (1,100 feet high) and find an array of wild flowers to complement the superb panorama of the islands. Roadways and paths make good walks if you do not care to climb. Rocky promontories, good for clambering, jumping, and sliding, project into the water at the end of the park beach. Those with dinghies find countless small coves to explore.

If you do not like setting your hook or mooring close to other boats, there are less populous anchorages near the inner north shore of Parker Island and in Payne Bay just inside Phillimore Point. And Montague Harbour Marina, south of the dock, has floats. But we have never found the massing of small craft in the big shallow sweep near the wharf at the park uncomfortable. In fact, one night's stop should be enough to demonstrate to you why many boating families head for Montague Harbour, drop anchor, and stay as long as their vacations last. On a recent midsummer visit we counted sixteen boats at anchor, fishing poles protruding from most of them. Dinghies plied here and there over the smooth water. In cockpits, on bows, and on the long narrow beach, people relaxed under a warm sun.

Look twice at the beaches of the park, by the way. A white area marks the location of a kitchen midden, a spot where untold generations of Gulf Islands Indian tribes threw away oyster, abalone, and clam shells after feasting here. Bleached by the sun, these broken shells sometimes gleam like new snow. They also prove that as long as man has lived in the Northwest, he has appreciated this gentle, protected bay.

Cruise Six takes you away from the beauties of Galiano Island's southerly shores. You set your course northwestward up the vast highway of Trincomali Channel, running between the deeply etched rocks and sandy niches of Grey Peninsula and Parker Island. You may encounter chop in the channel—we always do. We have tried crossing to the other side of Trincomali, but the wind is usually blowing straight up the wide water from the southeast, so there is no lee shore. But it does seem to help if you hug the waterline and stay out of midchannel.

This course gives you a wide view of the islands, large and small, and there are many attractive things to see along the way. Galiano itself bulks over you like a long, straight-sided levee. It rises to a harsh ridge, but on a shelflike shoulder about halfway up the bluff there are signs of habitation. Here a road some eighteen miles long parallels your course, and you will glimpse an occasional car, a house, many glorious old madronas, and a mile-long stand of tall, shadowy, white-trunked trees that must surely be birches.

Opposite you, forming the southwest shore of Trincomali Channel, is the long, solid coast of Salt Spring Island, which you will be able to examine more closely if you follow Cruise Seven. Today it simply forms a background for the series of small islands that are

Galiano Island

combed out northwest of Parker Island and the similar but larger chain of Wallace and the Secretary Islands.

Most interesting of all these lesser, wooded shapes are the Ballingall Islets (named for an officer who served aboard H.M.S. *Trincomalee*). Because seabirds find the tiny islands safe enough for nesting, British Columbia has designated them a provincial nature park. The little pigeon guillemot makes his home here. Both the pelagic and the double-crested cormorant have established thriving colonies on the islets, building thick nests of sticks that are visible from the water as you slowly, quietly idle your boat past them.

Beyond the Ballingalls you follow the Galiano shore for several miles, with little but your thoughts to draw your attention from it. Because it is enjoyable to ponder such matters, let us look at the local names again: British Royal Navy labels on the inside, Spanish labels on the great barrier island that is your guide-on to starboard. Ballingall is English, *Trincomalee* (hence Trincomali) is Ceylonese and reflects that profound and profitable preoccupation Britain had with the Indian subcontinent, a preoccupation that lasted for more than two centuries. The original Trincomalee is a beautiful natural harbor on the coast of Ceylon, and for many years it served as a principal naval port for Britain's India fleet.

The first major breakdown in the colonial relationship between England and India came in the bloody Sepoy Rebellion of 1857. Occurring at the same time the first Caucasian settlers reached the Gulf Islands, this empire-shaking event must have been one of the most important developments of the nineteenth century so far as the lords of trade in London were concerned. Preventing a repeat rebellion claimed first attention. There was no task on the North American continent so urgent as correcting whatever had gone wrong in Lucknow, Cawnpore, and Calcutta.

Out of India came names like that of Admiral Baynes's flagship, H.M.S. *Ganges,* and the H.M.S. *Trincomalee;* and from these vessels, so important to the Gulf Islands, came the name of the principal town on Salt Spring Island, Ganges, and the name of this channel you are cruising.

The old Spanish explorers, whose own empire crumbled while Britain's grew fat, might get ironic satisfaction from the sight of Galiano dominating the view from Trincomali. Unlike the heights on many of the other islands, Galiano's spine supports few trees. It thrusts bare red and brown slabs of stone into the sky, well above the tips of conifers that stand on its lower flanks.

The most attractive moorage on this island's long coast is in Retreat Cove, where a good-sized government wharf is half hidden behind Retreat Island in a quiet, idyllic little bay that invites you to tie up and stay a while. This is an optional stop, more useful to sailboats than to powerboats (which will probably reach Retreat Cove well before lunchtime). However, the charm of this small bay and the fact that few visiting yachtsmen have bothered to locate it may well induce you to go in and have a look. The cove is not considered a safe moorage if a strong westerly wind is blowing, but then none of the

Fishing boats in Porlier Pass

coast of Galiano is friendly in the face of a westerly. But you are not likely to venture forth on Cruise Six in a gale out of the west, are you?

Porlier Pass is the next feature of interest in this increasingly less populated mass of islands. It is the middle gateway between the Strait of Georgia and the inner Gulf Islands channels. Gabriola Passage to the north and Active Pass to the south carry much more traffic, but the rugged headlands of Porlier Pass present by far the most dramatic picture of the three. The Spanish explorers Valdes and Galiano first penetrated the outer Gulf Islands through Porlier Pass rather than through one of the more open passages. It happened in 1792, the third summer of Spanish exploration inside the Strait of Juan de Fuca. This year they were sharing the waters with the English expedition under Vancouver, and with this competition their hope of being first to find the Northwest Passage had lessened so they explored less hurriedly. When full sails had carried the *Sutil* and the *Mexicana* through the narrow gateway to the spot where you now find yourself, their officers and men took time to marvel at the array of islands that are visible from this vantage point.

Aware of the navigational hazards of the inside waterways (particularly unpredictable winds) and having no immediate interest in charting the complexity of channels on all sides, the Spaniards came about and returned through Porlier Pass to the strait. It was not easy. Strong currents of up to nine knots and many half-submerged rocks presented constant dangers. On the plus side, however, was their encounter with friendly Indians living in the pass, who greeted them warmly and came out in canoes to offer items of food to the struggling schooners.

As you look through Porlier Pass at a series of rocky points reaching in from both sides to constrict it, you can understand the Spaniards' problems. They were luckier by far than the crew of the tug *Peggy McNeill* of our own century. This vessel got caught by the swift currents of the pass in 1923 and overturned, spilling her men into the sea. Later, in 1938, a steel workboat called the *Point Grey* rammed a rock here and was lost, having given nearly forty years of service to the seaborne commerce of British Columbia.

These losses of the past do not dim the enthusiasm of today's fishermen who congregate in great numbers, especially in July, to intercept the salmon that are making their way through Porlier Pass and heading for their spawning grounds across the Strait of Georgia.

Now it is time for you to turn away from the pass and the fishermen to cross Trincomali Channel. Its width is substantial at this point, but Reid Island lies like a great stepping stone between you and Thetis Island on the far side. Be sure to angle well north of Reid Island in order to clear the reef that is visible as Rose Islets. You should not approach Rose Islets very closely in any case, because they have been set aside as an ecological preserve. Pleasure boats skimming near them are likely to disturb the breeding grounds of marine wildlife.

The solid chunk of Reid Island is privately owned and already subdivided. One day it may wear a cluster of houses, but at present it looks virtually untouched by man. Its heavily indented southwestern shore is worth viewing up close sometime, but it is far enough off our course to be bypassed for the present. Instead, you are heading for Pilkey Point on Thetis Island. For safety we recommend that you swing up around the marker buoy north of Miami Islet, thereby avoiding reef and rocks. You may want to double back south for an exploratory run along the inlets and headlands of North Cove on Thetis Island. Lying open to a wide expanse of water, this shoreline suffers from adverse winds, so few skippers linger here, despite the lonely beauty of the place.

You are now at the northern end of one long, broad, and rather low-lying landmass, which is divided into two islands by a thin skin of water, or "waist," that dries at low tide. The land north of this waist is Thetis Island, that to the south is Kuper Island, an Indian reserve. Leading into the waist on the southwestern side is the long, narrow, well-protected inlet called Telegraph Harbour, which is our next destination.

Swinging wide around Fraser Point to avoid the rocks near you, set a course that parallels the southwest shore of Thetis and begin heading generally southward for the first time today. You may be interested to note how few people are to be seen on this pleasant, smiling island. Not many permanent residents have settled on Thetis, even though it is fairly large and is served by a small ferry. Two reasons may be that farming so far from a market probably is not profitable and the nearest towns where one might find employment—Chemainus and Ladysmith—are too far away for comfortable commuting.

You are now running down the second of the larger channels that divide the northern Gulf Islands. This is Stuart Channel, which, after a merging with Trincomali north of Thetis Island, lies south southeast all the way to Sansum Narrows. Along its entire length, Vancouver Island forms a broken and populous western shore. The contrast between the shores is distinct. At a distance to starboard, you are seeing twentieth-century industrial development, log booms, mills, and houses that spread in wide sweeps up the hilly shoreline. Nearby to port, you see trees, some birds, and the rocky waterline—a scene virtually unchanged for thousands of years. Missing are the dugout canoes paddled by Indians, who a century ago half lived on these waters and moved about them with far more confidence than we in our large, electronically equipped vessels can ever hope to have.

As you proceed southward, a broadening of Stuart Channel indicates that you are opposite the busy Ladysmith Harbour on Vancouver Island. You may think of investigating, but by now, unless you lunched in transit or at Retreat Cove, you are undoubtedly hungry. The best plan is to turn from these distant built-up shores of the big island and, instead, make directly for Telegraph Harbour, whose entrance is no more than two miles ahead. It lies beyond the small islands that now appear to block your way. These landfalls—Scott, Dayman, and Hudson—shelter Preedy Harbour, which has a small government wharf and the ferry landing for Thetis Island, from which car ferries operating out of Chemainus carry Thetis Islanders across to Vancouver Island.

You can make a temporary stop in Preedy Harbor if you like. Our own preference is to pull out around Scott, Dayman, and Hudson (named for officers who served aboard H.M.S. *Thetis*) and enter Telegraph Harbour. As you curve in behind Foster Point, you will see a wide acreage on Kuper Island where the trees have been cleared. In the clearing, not far from the water, is an unexpected sight: a tall building with a cupola. It is the kind of structure that one might well expect to see on the other side of Stuart Channel, but not here in wilderness surroundings. The building is a school, built to educate the children of Indian families that reside on the Kuper Island reserve. A private wharf leads out from the school's terrace, but you pass it and head much farther in. Now you can see where the harbor narrows and, like a rounded fingertip, ends.

Telegraph Harbour is one of two spots suggested for this night's moorage, because the uninterrupted run from Montague Harbour is long enough to be tiring, and you or your crew are probably anxious to call it quits for the day. Something to eat, a dinghy exploration of the harbor and the shores, perhaps a look up the little dredged channel that allows small boats to ease through to Clam Bay at high tide—all these sound good, and the rest of the afternoon will go quickly.

However, if you have been moving right along and averaging some twelve knots on power, the cruise thus far may not have exhausted your zest for the day. In that case, you might lunch here and proceed to Maple Bay for the night. The course from Telegraph Harbour to Maple Bay is direct and open, and will take you another hour or two. The distance is about twelve nautical miles.

It may be well to comment now on marina stops. Private commercial marinas frequently offer the best moorage that is available to cruising families. We like parks and small sheltered coves, as you may have guessed by now. But on a trip through the Gulf Islands, where there are even fewer built-up communities than in the San Juans, commercial marinas are almost like crossroads towns on an automobile trip. They provide emergency repairs and supplies, usually a small restaurant or café, and fuel. In some cases they even offer a playground for children, not all of whom can spend endless hours gazing into tide pools. You can anchor at the head of Telegraph Harbour, if you like, in dependable holding ground, well sheltered from the winds. But the two marinas in this handsome, narrow cul-de-sac have a good deal to offer.

The older and larger of the two, Telegraph Harbour Marina, is located at the head of the inlet. It is prepared to supply things as various as engine repair and children's swings. You can count on doing your laundry and taking a shower. You can plug into dockside power, buy groceries and snacks, or rent bicycles for a quick tour into the interior of the island.

Thetis Island Marina's location, part way along the harbor's graceful curve, is peculiarly attractive. It nestles behind a wall of pilings that protects it from the wash of passing boats. This marina is a friendly place, where the owner attempts to greet all arriving boats in person. It has a first-rate dining room, a well-stocked grocery store, and numerous other amenities. Despite the reference to the wash of transiting boats, you will not find crowds in Telegraph Harbour—nothing like the crowds at city marinas, large or small. There is a quiet peace about the inlet. Both establishments are well sheltered from storms inside the wooded arms that enclose Telegraph Harbour.

One of our favorite stops in this area is Maple Bay Marina, located at the head of Maple Bay in Bird's Eye Cove. Maple Bay opens off Sansum Narrows, the channel that runs between Salt Spring and Vancouver islands. The marina is not actually on a Gulf island, of course. But Vancouver Island is so important to the smaller islands in its lee that one cannot always discuss them separately. The interplay between city and wilderness, between markets and fishing banks, between vacationers and vacation villages is so complete that it seems as if one could not exist without the other. Particularly at those points where the small islands lie close to Vancouver Island, it is pleasant to sample both shores of the waterway that separates them. Maple Bay, for example, is of primary importance to the Gulf Islands because many yachtsmen from Victoria use it as a springboard to island boating. With permanent or summer-long moorage at Maple Bay Marina, these boatmen have only to drive up-island and board their boats to be instantly in the heart of the water wonderland.

The Mai Tai, located on a narrow shelf of rock beside Maple Bay Marina's grocery store, is a first-class, Polynesian-style restaurant, offering a touch of comfort and luxury to boatmen who have spent several days roughing it. The marina itself is well supplied with the usual amenities.

If you prefer, you can anchor at the head of Bird's Eye Cove, beyond the marina. Here the narrowing canyon has an ethereal loveliness. Wisps of fog caught high up in mountain valleys above you complement small, limpid lagoons below; contained by close-crowding boulders, these pools of water reflect the overhanging peaks and scudding clouds. Herons stalk along their shores.

If you wish to stop overnight at one of the three marinas, remember to reserve space ahead, especially on summer weekends. Note that none of them has sleeping units ashore, so those who cannot sleep on their boats must find other moorage. One alternative is Vesuvius Bay on Salt Spring Island just north of Sansum Narrows and Booth Bay. Here you can anchor your boat and walk a short distance up the road to a pleasant motel. Unfortunately, campsites are few in this particular area.

Morning brings you fresh and open-eyed to your encounter with one of the handsomest passages in all the islands, Gulf or San Juan. Sansum Narrows describes an irregular cross between Salt Spring Island and Vancouver Island. If you stayed the night in Maple Bay, you have already entered a part of the narrows and gone far enough to be awed by its distant reaches, where the water runs between mountainous walls dropping sheer to the shore. In parts it is a high-walled canyon, and water depths here can be astonishing, considering the narrowness of the passage: as deep as one hundred fathoms in some places.

A curious quality of Sansum Narrows, with its arms reaching into Burgoyne Bay and Maple Bay, is that the land looks almost empty—a wilderness on the Salt Spring side—and yet the water is covered with boats. Off Bold Bluff you may see as many as thirty small skiffs, each occupant handling one or two fishing lines. Larger boats ignore the through traffic to troll back and forth across the channel, gambling their expensive gear that you will take the trouble to go around it. Sailboats tack in the odd winds of the narrows, and rowboats dart out from tiny bights, causing you to watch both water and chart more intently than at any time since Active Pass.

Meanwhile, above you the silent, wooded cliffs rise into the sky; mountaintops over two thousand feet high loom near the partly shaded waters, and rock outcrops support thin carpets of grass or moss. From Burgoyne Bay on Salt Spring you can look up to the edge of Mount Maxwell Park and see only a few signs of life. It is dangerous to creep close to the edge up there; park visitors are warned to stand well back.

Cutting some five miles through these bluffs, Sansum Narrows ends at Separation Point on Vancouver Island. At several places along this spectacular stretch of water, the Canadian government has constructed small wharves. You will identify them by their red paint. These are excellent places for brief stops, or longer stops if you have time. Some rather rough mountain roads connect them to the interior of Salt Spring Island. Their floats may have room for three or four boats to moor at one time. There is one such wharf in Burgoyne Bay, another at Musgrave Landing. The latter, in the lee of the small, exquisite projection of Musgrave Point, has a setting that few other moorings can rival. It also has the advantage of being isolated and uncrowded.

From Sansum Narrows your course curves around the foot of Mount Tuam on Salt Spring Island and then through Satellite Channel. If you took Cruise Three, you will recognize the landmarks of Moses Point and Wain Rock off the tip of Saanich Peninsula. Now, if you hug the Salt Spring shore, you will be able to appreciate the sheer heights of the great massif that rises overhead. It is not surprising that its peak was a focal point for Indian myth and legend in the centuries before European settlers arrived. Mount Tuam was visible for long distances and was considered a holy place, seat of the sun god. The canoe folk named it *Chu-an,* which means "facing the sea" in the language of the Cowichan tribe.

Salmon leaping all around the base of this mountain will explain the presence of the fishing boats you passed this morning and those up ahead, so motionless they look painted on the water.

Around the bend is Fulford Harbour, which makes a good stop for lunch. A midchannel course will enable you to avoid the rocks along its northeastern shore, but be wary of accumulations of driftwood as you approach the dock. If you are expecting a substantial town at Fulford Harbour, you will be disappointed. There is a public wharf, standing long and narrow on pilings, and a landing, which sees frequent arrivals and departures of the big, flat-bottomed ferries. Wash from a ferry keeps water stirred up for quite a while; so mooring at the small, outer floats can be troublesome. A more sheltered spot lies farther on, in the quiet waters behind the ferry landing.

Houses, a market, a church on the hill, a small post office, and a coffee shop are pretty well all there is to the town, except for some marine repair shops near the docks. Roads out of Fulford Harbour circle around the head of the inlet, giving you a fine walk through beautiful pastoral countryside and chances for memorable photography or a handsome addition to your sketchbook.

The last leg of Cruise Six takes you from Fulford Harbour,

around Eleanor and Beaver points, into Ganges Harbour. As you pass Beaver Point, you may see a few people, or even a few sheep, on the grassy slopes that rise above the shoreline. This area became Ruckle Park in 1974, as a result of the generosity of the Ruckle family, which has owned a large farm here for a hundred years. Provisions in the donation grant permit the family to continue grazing sheep and farming the land while park facilities are being developed. The point is a favorite spot with artists, nature lovers, and that peculiar species of the islands, the driftwood craftsmen.

A small bay just around the corner from Beaver Point was the site of a large commercial wharf in days gone by—the principal connection between Salt Spring Island and the outside world, where steamers landed passengers and supplies. But today no structures remain to mark the spot.

The course from here to Ganges Harbour, where you will probably want to spend the night, is rather simple. Russell and other offshore islands are easily avoided, and your only concern is to enter between the double line of day beacons that marks the municipal marina at Ganges. If you prefer, you can go east around the main part of the town and tie to the government wharf behind it.

Ganges is the junction point for Cruise Seven, but you may be planning to turn homeward from this stop. If so, a good course lies southeast to Beaver Point along the Salt Spring shore; then, crossing Swanson Channel, it takes you down the Oaks Bluff coast of North Pender Island. Just short of Bedwell Harbour you can cut across Haro Strait toward Turn Point on Stuart Island. Beyond is the familiar crossing to Roche Harbor for customs. If you are running out of time, you can probably make it all the way back to Anacortes in one day on power; we once hurried home from Ganges to Bellingham via Roche Harbor and Harney Channel, taking a flu-ridden child to her own bed. We had choppy water, as usual, and we rarely went as much as fifteen knots, even hurrying; yet we arrived home in little more than half a day.

Cruise
Seven

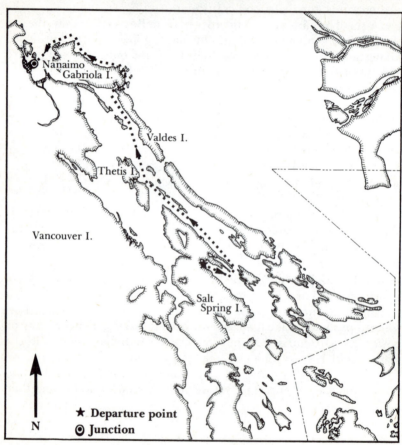

Do not use for navigation.
Use Canadian Hydrographic Service Small Craft Chart 3310

Ganges through Gabriola to Nanaimo

Point of departure: Ganges Harbour
Course: via Captain Passage, Trincomali Channel, Houstoun Passage, Pylades Channel, Gabriola Passage, Strait of Georgia, Fairway Channel, Nanaimo Harbour
Stops: Long Harbour, Walker Hook, Fernwood Point, Degnen Bay, Silva Bay
Length of cruise: approximately 47 nautical miles to Nanaimo
Duration on power: 2 days
Duration on sail: 3 to 4 days
Overnight moorage:
  First night: Degnen Bay or Silva Bay
  Second night: Nanaimo
Junction with Cruise Eight: Nanaimo

Settlers' Shores

Until now, each of the cruises described in this book has executed a loop that returned you to some spot reasonably near its point of departure or to a customs dock in familiar territory, from which you could return directly to your home port.

Cruises Seven and Eight, however, encompass waters so distant from the original departure point of Anacortes that it will be best to think of them as a linked pair that should be undertaken together. Abandoning the loop pattern, Cruise Seven ends at the northernmost destination covered by this book. Cruise Eight takes you from that point, along a different route than Cruise Seven's, back to U.S. customs on San Juan Island.

We begin at Ganges on Salt Spring Island, which to our way of thinking is the heart of the Gulf Islands group. For thorough exploration, this charming town deserves two or three days of your time, rather than an overnight visit, and once you make its acquaintance you will probably come back as often as possible.

A commemorative waterfront park, just above the municipal dock, is lined for two city blocks with immense planter boxes, crowded in summer with petunias and geraniums and other bright blooms. It also features benches and a small playground, much used by the younger set. Behind the park is the business section of the town—a jumble of markets, old-fashioned shops, real-estate offices, and service stations, separated from each other by a baffling maze of streets called a "circle." There is nothing standardized about Ganges. It will remind you of no other town; yet it makes little apparent effort to look unusual. Perhaps because chain stores have not moved in, each shop is clearly one you have never seen. The buildings—plain, unadorned, foursquare frame structures with covered porches—evoke the image of an old-west town. Curbs are of irregular heights, and the solid-looking bank, set in the midst of the town, seems a misfit.

At Mouat's, a large, well-stocked general store, you can buy a very wide variety of goods and supplies at reasonable prices. (Once, having left a crew member's duffel bag behind, we duplicated its whole contents from Mouat's without breaking the vacation budget.) While there, be sure you wander down into the basement, now called

Ganges Harbour on Salt Spring Island

Mouat's Mall. It will give you a hint of the historic importance of Salt Spring Island, in the development of which the Mouat family played an important role. The corridors of the mall are lined with old photographs, carefully preserved and enlarged. You see an earlier Ganges, with lumber schooners, turn-of-the-century excursion boats, and coal-burning cargo vessels docking at the wharf.

It was in Ganges that we first fully appreciated the early-day importance of the Royal Navy in the Gulf Islands. Talking with the editor of a widely distributed regional newspaper, the *Gulf Islands Driftwood,* we heard an enthusiastic account of H.M.S. *Ganges,* the great vessel for which the town was named. She was a sailing ship, all teak, and carried eighty-four guns. Built in Bombay in the late eighteenth century, she saw 150 years of service and finally ended up in England as a training ship for recruits in the Royal Navy. Along about the middle of her career, she served four years based at Victoria as Rear Admiral R. L. Baynes's flagship. Her duty then was, in part, to provide protection for the first of the settlers who came to Salt Spring Island. Baynes, as commander of the Queen's naval forces in the Pacific, also had other things to do; so the *Ganges* was not always visible in Salt Spring waters. *Plumper,* the survey ship, and *Satellite,* and smaller naval vessels came and went, but it is the idea of the great man-of-war, *Ganges,* with her complement of 840 fighting men, that still arouses enthusiasm in residents of the Gulf Islands.

In the Ganges waterfront park, a prominent stone monument reads: "H.M.S. Ganges. This cairn with seat was erected July 1st 1967 by H.M.S. Ganges Chapter I.O.D.E. Inset is the seatback from the captain's galley (or Gig) of H.M.S. Ganges, the last sailing ship of the Royal Navy, after whom this harbour was named. She patrolled these waters 1857–1861."

Do those last dates ring a bell? They are four of the years during which the international boundary was in dispute, a time when no nation possessed the waters that run between the San Juan and Gulf islands. It was 1859, remember, when all available units of the Royal Navy were called on to focus their attention on Griffin Bay at San Juan Island, to run out their guns, and to hold their fire. At that very same time, Salt Spring Island was seeing its first wave of permanent settlement.

All told, the 1850s were an important time to this whole section of the Northwest. Seattle's first white settlers arrived in 1851 and 1852; Bellingham was settled between 1852 and 1857; Port Townsend dates from 1851 and Coupeville from 1852; British Columbia Province was founded in 1858. Only Victoria, West Coast headquarters of the Hudson's Bay Company, could count a resident population in the 1840s, and officials there noted the influx of settlers into other areas with some alarm. To put the situation into perspective, one needs to remember the tensions building toward civil war in the United States, the Fraser Valley gold rush in British Columbia in 1858, and the presence in Bellingham, Victoria, and throughout the islands of transient miners, whose mere presence influenced the decisions of governors and admirals alike.

The first settlers of Salt Spring Island, who arrived in 1857, were nine blacks from Kentucky and other parts of the southern United States. They were only a few of the eight hundred black people who planned to immigrate to Vancouver Island, some six hundred of whom arrived before and during the gold rush. These were free people, not escaped slaves, but they left the United States because of the worsening climate there for blacks as the Civil War approached. They built cabins and began clearing small farms on Salt Spring Island near Vesuvius Bay. Encounters with Indians, particularly raiding Haidas and Bella Bellas who were looking for slaves, were not encouraging, but they persisted, and their descendents still live on Salt Spring Island. After them came immigrants and settlers from Scotland, England, Australia, other parts of Canada, and the United States.

Farming was the principal concern of Salt Spring residents for most of its history: there were apple and pear orchards, dairy and poultry farms, pastures for sheep, and plowed fields yielding barley, oats, and potatoes. At first, farmers could profitably export these crops to the rapidly growing population on Vancouver Island—again ships were the lifeline. This time the side-wheeler *Beaver* was the most important vessel. But economics eventually caught up with island farming enterprises. Mainland and Vancouver Island farmers could sell the same commodities for less, and today Salt Spring produces scarcely enough food to feed her own population of some four thousand people. Concerned in the past primarily with the land, this island is increasingly looking to the sea.

Resorts have sprung up all over Salt Spring—twenty or more, ranging from a first-rate waterfront hotel to simple lakeside campsites. There are flourishing boat-rental establishments in Ganges Harbour, and Mouat's store has recently expanded its seventy-year-old enterprise, building a wide-windowed annex that faces directly on the water just north of the town's main street.

You should walk to the end of this bit of pavement and look at the timbers where deep-draft vessels used to tie up. To the left, identified by the familiar red paint, is the government wharf many boatmen tie to when Ganges' municipal wharf is full. They often find themselves sharing this moorage with a small seaplane or a deep water sailing vessel from San Francisco or Seattle.

See as much as possible of Ganges on the day you come into port. It is a good place to stock up on groceries, liquor, and fuel, and to partake of a shore meal or two. Next morning it will be time to set out for a taste of the northernmost Gulf Islands—and Nanaimo.

When you leave Ganges Harbour you must move circumspectly down the center of its long inlet. Tempting passages among the Chain Islands are safe for local boatmen; however, even rowboats have been known to get hung up on the rocks between Goat Island and the Sisters. Once past Second Sister Island, you can make for Scott Point, to the northeast, in a nice easy curve. As you near it the lovely, still waters of Welbury Bay, off the port beam, may attract your attention. Enclosed by high ground on three sides, this small basin is a serene and glistening backwater; above it, at the far end of the bay, you may be able to see part of a small park with steep, winding paths and frequent benches. Here travelers stroll and perch, gazing seaward, as they wait for the British Columbia ferries—today's waterborne lifeline for Salt Spring Island.

As you round Scott Point, you may come upon one of these ferries making its stately approach up Long Harbour to the out-of-town landing that now serves Ganges. Since your course also lies up Long Harbour, to be safe you will probably wait until its passengers are disembarking before you go beyond it up the deep, narrow sliver of water that stretches between beautifully wooded bluffs far into the island. A glance at the chart will show you that Salt Spring and nearby

Welbury Bay on Salt Spring Island

Prevost Island are both indented by a series of similar deep, narrow bays—drowned valleys—and each stretches a set of rocky promontories toward the other. Yachtsmen who like to anchor in quiet coves in the hope of finding solitude should explore such places as James Bay, Selby Cove, and Annette Inlet on the little-developed island of Prevost. If a bit more sociable, boatmen can put down an anchor in Long Harbour itself, past the ferry landing. Well protected, it is also a well-loved anchorage, and clusters of boats are usually found there. Your excursion up Long Harbour is intended merely to show you the attractions of this area, with its overhanging trees and sheltered shallows. A stop, which means anchoring, is optional and depends entirely on the amount of time you have, but a dinghy exploration to the shallow headwaters of this inlet can provide a rewarding revelation of natural beauty.

On the southwest side of Long Harbour is a charming complex of buildings and wharves that were once a commercial marina but are now an outport for a mainland yacht club. As such, they no longer have accommodations for transient yachtsmen.

Now you retrace your course out of Long Harbour. At Nose Point you enter Captain Passage, where an attractive array of small promontories reaches out in overlapping outlines from Prevost Island. Taking them to starboard, you cruise through Captain Passage and come to an old friend: Trincomali Channel! This time, however, you are on the far side from Galiano Island. Directly across the water to the northeast you can see the small opening that leads to Montague Harbour, and side by side next to it are the twin peaks of Sutil Mountain and Mount Galiano. If you are at all like us, you will pause to marvel at how unfamiliar familiar landmarks can look when seen from a new vantage point. From here the course lies parallel to the shore of Salt Spring as you head a little west of north, up Trincomali. Be sure to check your chart for Atkins Reef, which extends southeastward from Walker Hook. The best plan is to swing wide around this row of submerged rocks, using the elbow of Walker Hook as an indicator of your location. Local boatmen cross the reef at any number of places, but it is not marked clearly enough for strangers to negotiate safely, so we avoid it.

Walker Hook is another optional moorage, a beautiful stop on a leisurely cruise. Today, you will probably want to do no more than pull into the mouth of it, cautiously, because of submerged rocks, and idle there for a brief moment while you enjoy the appealing little enclosure. Driftwood of all sizes lies in haphazard heaps around the tree-framed shallows, and at low tide moss-covered mud emerges from the receding waters. At such times the floating drift, from great logs to leafy branches, comes to rest on the mud, making curious patterns over the whole dried basin, and you may feel an irrational desire to add your footprints to the composition.

A short run on up the Salt Spring coast brings you to Fernwood Point, where you will find a long wharf built well out over the water on tall pilings. It offers a small float.

This is a public wharf, and it makes a good lunch stop on today's run. We suggest not only that you tie up here but that you also take a picnic lunch ashore. As the tall pilings suggest, the land at Fernwood Point stands well above the shoreline as a kind of low mesa. This part of the island differs strikingly from its southern section, which is studded with mountains. One of the island's roads runs along the modest elevation at Fernwood Point, and a thin line of sandy beach rims the shore below. The road is separated from the land's edge by a ribbon of shaded, grassy parkland, where a picnic table stands. So spread your feast and munch away in relaxed somnolence. If there are children with you, they can scramble up and down the steep bank above the beach, wade and even swim in the clear waters near the wharf's pilings, and ride deadheads to their heart's content.

Afterward you can set off on a rather longer stretch of cruising that takes you north up Houstoun Passage, past the Secretary Islands, with their several narrow passages, and out beyond the tip of Norway Island into the main Trincomali Channel once again. Taking picturesque Penelakut Spit well to port, you find yourself passing Reid Island on the side opposite to the one you saw in Cruise Six. Now you can appreciate its attraction for builders of vacation homes. Gently

Walker Hook on Salt Spring Island

concave and slightly elevated, this side of Reid offers an unsurpassed view of the many intriguing landfalls between Norway Island and Panther Point on Wallace Island.

Next our cruise cuts across Trincomali on a northerly diagonal and then runs northwesterly up Pylades Channel. At first bordered to the northeast by the steep slopes of Valdes Island rising to Mexicana Hill, and then by the more gradual inclines of the island's northern slopes, you see an almost unbroken shoreline running up ahead to Dibuxante Point. Valdes is in part an Indian reserve and has few marks of settlement on it. A short stretch of road near Blackberry Point is scarcely visible as you cruise by. To the west are the many fascinating shapes of smaller islands: Pylades, Ruxton, De Courcy, Link, and—obscured by the others—low-lying Mudge, off in the distance. As you near Dibuxante Point and the entrance to Gabriola Passage, you will observe a number of boats, perhaps even a tug pulling a log boom, headed northwestward for an invisible opening between Gabriola Island and Mudge. This is False Narrows, an attractive passage, which looks more alarming on the chart than it really is.

For some it is a well-marked shortcut to Nanaimo. But our cruise encompasses some even more attractive spots on the far side of Gabriola Passage, so you head around the light marking its entrance and go eastward into this beautiful passage.

From this point, you can see straight through it. The rocky fringes in Gabriola Passage are much less menacing than those we observed in Porlier, and it is easy to understand why so many Vancouver yachtsmen prefer this opening for their doorway to the inner Gulf Islands watercourses. As in Active Pass, tidal action through these narrows is substantial, and swift currents can cause trouble for slow-moving, deep-keel boats. Try to time your transit for slack water, staying away from both ebb and flood tides.

On your left as you enter the passage is an attractive inlet named Degnen Bay, and if it is growing late, you can settle in here for the night amidst beautiful surroundings. Its western edges are shallow and hazardous for an overnight stay, but to the northeast you will find a fine public wharf with larger-than-usual floats, and beyond them is good anchorage. This end of the bay is rimmed with handsome cliffs of solid stone, in colors ranging from rust red to moss green, and resident belted kingfishers keep the air alive with their cries as they dive for an evening meal.

A small road runs from the big Degnen Bay wharf along the shore of the harbor and then inland to a junction with the main Gabriola circle road. It makes a beautiful walk in late afternoon, as colors begin to change on the water. One of the few places in these islands where you will find deciduous trees massed near a shoreline, the road is especially attractive in spring and fall. Colors of the changing autumn leaves reflected in the water rival the fall displays of New England.

You may, however, prefer to complete your run through Gabriola Passage before settling in tonight. Much depends on when the tides are running. In two places where Gabriola and Valdes islands almost meet, the passage constricts tightly. You ease through the wider of the two spots as you round Dibuxante Point, but up ahead is the narrower, formed by Josef Point on Gabriola and Cordero Point on Valdes. Here currents swirl visibly against the outthrust rock.

After you clear Josef Point, the pass widens to a broad pool. You will head around Rogers Reef and turn north for the channel between two lights on tall supports, the starboard light on Breakwater Island, the port light on Rogers Reef. Ahead, at the other end of this channel, is another light, which you take to port as you curve northwestward into Commodore Passage.

Slowly now: you are almost at the entrance to Silva Bay. Silva Bay is a beautiful little basin that has several approaches, and once you know them, you will enter confidently by the unmarked ones. But for today, enter by way of Commodore Passage, and watch for a small channel to port where yet another light marks the primary entrance to the bay. Ever since setting off through Gabriola Passage you have turned left and left and left again, until your course, if drawn on a chart, would look like a huge fishhook. Now, facing southwest, you run on into Silva Bay.

There are many places to anchor in this charming harbor, and you will see a scattering of vessels already swinging on hooks. You can follow their example, or you can head for the big line of floats that marks Silva Bay Resort Hotel. If you are in the mood for some self-indulgence, this is your place. On the dock at the top of the gangway, there is a hot-dog stand named the Sloop, a pub (serving beer and hard cider), a laundry, showers, toilets, and a trash-deposit station. Up the slope a short distance, steps lead to a dining room and cocktail lounge (beer, cider, and mixed drinks). These two large, freshly decorated facilities open onto a wide, paved deck that overlooks a heated swimming pool, the floats, and the bay. More like Rosario Resort than anything else you have seen on these cruises, Silva Bay Resort's deck and terrace are elevated high enough so you can look over the tops of the breakwater islands toward the mountains of the distant British Columbia mainland.

The resort's restaurant has excellent food and the prices are moderate. Comfortable rooms are available in the main building, if you prefer a night ashore. Should you choose to stay aboard your boat at the floats of Silva Bay Resort Hotel, prepare for an interesting evening. Impromptu songfests, augmented by the sounds of a guitarist or a bagpiper, are likely to begin once the sun sets. Here you can be party to a very special style of wholehearted fun, as a crowd gathers round the cockpit of a boat where songsters are holding forth. One by one the onlookers join in the chorus, to continue, sometimes, well into the night.

The rounded basin of Silva Bay contains another resort, older and smaller, but pleasant, called Page Marina. And Silva Bay Ship-yard, also in the basin, is equipped to help you with any mechanical crisis that your boat is likely to experience; they build boats, supply dry storage, and haul out tall sailboats on their Travelift. Vessels up to two hundred tons can be handled on their marine ways.

Across the basin from Silva Bay Resort Hotel is an island branch of the Royal Vancouver Yacht Club, and you will see dozens of masts marking the spot.

In the morning, you need not rise early unless you want to. The day's cruise is shorter than most in order to get you to Nanaimo at an hour when moorage will be easy to find. You will probably complete the run in about two hours if you have power.

The exit from Silva Bay through Commodore Passage and northward among the Flat Top Islands is narrow but unimpeded. Shining rock formations, carved by the tides, decorate this little pass, giving it a remarkable, chiseled beauty, which you can briefly scan before emerging into the Strait or Gulf of Georgia.

Entering the strait is almost like entering open ocean, with a huge expanse of water stretching away in every direction, often characterized by ocean-type swells or chop. The strait can be quite smooth, however. The last time we made this cruise a light southeasterly was blowing, the water on the strait rippled gently, and we enjoyed as fine a run as the fairest of fair-weather sailors could want. We will wish the same for you.

Running westward and northward parallel to the shore of Gabriola Island, you will be almost even with the mouths of the Fraser River across the Strait of Georgia. On a clear day, the snowy range that rises abruptly above Vancouver to the east seems to fill the sky. Gabriola's own mass, quite near at hand, towers over your boat in a uniformly etched cliff that is sheered away as vertically as a stone wall. Along the crest of the cliff stand fringes of evergreens, mostly fir, and at its base is the familiar scattering of tumbled rocks that lines so many of the Gulf Islands.

You leave the strait rather soon, much sooner than if you had crossed it from the city of Vancouver. Tiny Entrance Island, displaying the red roofs and white walls of a major lighthouse installation, lies off Orlebar Point, with Forwood Channel between. You run this channel and turn again to follow the Gabriola shore until you round Tinson and Malaspina points. From here you can see Nanaimo, sheltering behind Newcastle and Protection islands. McKay Channel—carefully marked with nun and can buoys and a very substantial lighthouse at Gallows Point—is the approach you follow into Nanaimo Harbour.

Our first arrival in Nanaimo was in the late afternoon one August day, and we can testify that even a city with a large municipal docking facility may run low on space in the summer. The Commercial Inlet Boat Basin, behind a small promontory to your left as you near the city's shoreline, was jammed. We recommend that you plan to arrive by 1400 hours at the latest. When you have found a slip and made fast your lines, you are ready to explore Nanaimo, the Bastion City of Vancouver Island.

We begin Cruise Eight with a description of this amiable, bustling town that sweeps up the sides of gentle Mount Benson like a tidal bore.

Cruise
Eight

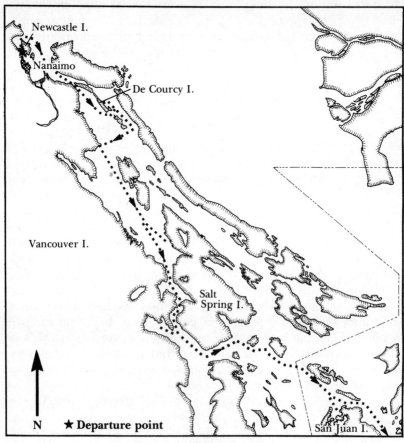

Newcastle I.

Nanaimo

De Courcy I.

Vancouver I.

Salt
Spring I.

N ★ Departure point

San Juan I.

Do not use for navigation.
Use NOAA 18423, Folio Small-Craft Chart, and Canadian Hydrographic
Service Small Craft Chart 3310

Nanaimo to Roche Harbor

Point of departure: Departure Bay

Course: via Northumberland Channel, Dodd Narrows, Stuart Channel, Ruxton Passage, Pylades Channel, back to Stuart Channel, Sansum Narrows, Satellite Channel, Shute Passage, Prevost Passage, Haro Strait

Stops: Pirates Cove, Yellow Point (Ladysmith), Vesuvius or Genoa bays, Portland Island

Length of cruise: approximately 58 nautical miles to Roche Harbor

Duration on power: 2 or 3 days

Duration on sail: 3 to 5 days

Overnight moorage:
> First night: Pirates Cove
> Second night: Vesuvius or Genoa bays or Roche Harbor

This is the last of the eight cruises that are linked at junction points.

From Coal to Lime

Before settling in to enjoy Nanaimo there is one piece of planning that you should do. Take out your tide tables and calculate the times of tomorrow's slack water for Dodd Narrows, the slim passage that takes you most directly from Nanaimo to the inner Gulf Islands waters and starts you on Cruise Eight. The current in the narrows is so swift that transit should ordinarily be avoided unless you are near slack water. Remember that it takes an hour, more or less, to reach Dodd Narrows from Nanaimo. This chore completed, it is time to see the city.

Nanaimo deserves more than a fleeting visit. It is like Ganges, unique. If you can spare an extra day or two, you will be glad of the chance to explore this bright, vigorous town, interesting both for its colorful past and promising future.

We assume that you have moored for the night at Commercial Inlet Boat Basin, a government-supported small-craft harbor at the foot of Nanaimo's famous historical monument, the Bastion. Moorage here is low-cost, about half what you will pay in most commercial marinas. Three quarters of the basin is sheltered by high embankments. The wharfinger's office building, containing lavatories, showers, and an ice vending machine as well as the office, is central to the many finger piers. You reach it by a gangway that also leads up into the small memorial park around the Bastion, which stands white and sturdy and small on the bluff above. A second gangway leads from the floats to Nanaimo Harbour Park, a splendid new shopping center, complete with covered arcade and a multitude of shops ready to serve you. It is close by: you can replenish ship's stores in the Harbour Park mall and carry them back to your slip with little effort.

The wharfinger can be the most helpful official you will encounter in Nanaimo. When we last entered Commercial Inlet, the officer in charge was a cheerful, good-humored Scot-Canadian who admitted that he still thinks highly of the boating public after twenty-five years of experience working with it. Very reassuring.

From the graveled driveway next to the wharfinger's office, you can stroll along an attractive embankment promenade that rims the Nanaimo waterfront, linking up eventually with Georgia Park and its display of an ancient-style dugout canoe flanked by Indian totem poles. Beside the canoe is a sign that reads: "Squamish canoe. A fine example of a dugout canoe cut out of a cedar log in 1922 on Squamish Indian Reserve, Howe Sound. Acquired by Albert Wesley, Nanaimo Indian Reserve, in 1926, and given by him to Captain Higgs. Presented to the city of Nanaimo by Captain Higgs in 1937." If you examine the dugout, you will discover a sea serpent painted on the hull.

Only steps away from the dock is the Centennial Museum, which has some fine historical displays that illuminate Nanaimo's origins and its early coal-mining technology.

Much of central Nanaimo is in easy walking distance of Commercial Inlet, including places where you can dine well. Our favorite is the Malaspina Hotel, which overlooks the harbor and, among other items on its menu, offers English-style steak and kidney pie. The view from this hostelry is incredible because you are up on a high shelf in a position to see every boat, every small plane, every ferry that enters McKay Channel. Light from the setting sun colors each waterway and mountain with mauve and violet and pale yellow.

Once more, what about names? Malaspina Hotel commemorates a Spanish captain whose officers in 1792 led an expedition into these waters, exploring not only the harbor but the famous rock galleries that line an inlet of northern Gabriola Island. And Nanaimo? When the five hundred or so Coast Salish people who used to live around the bay gathered together, they were called *Snynemos,* meaning "the

Nanaimo on Vancouver Island

great and mighty people." Say it to yourself quickly and you can hear the derivation of Nanaimo.

Nanaimo also has a popular name: two, in fact. The first is Bastion City. As we have seen, the original Bastion occupies a prominent place on the embankment overlooking the harbor. It was a fortified blockhouse built and used by the Hudson's Bay Company. Small, distinctively octagonal in shape, and about thirty feet high, it reminds one of how meager the defenses were that sheltered newcomers to the Northwest only a little over a century ago.

The story of the Bastion is almost incredible. In the 1840s, when few non-Indians resided on Puget Sound or the Strait of Georgia, coal was shipped in from England for use in Victoria, which was then a thriving community representing the Hudson's Bay Company's westernmost activities. A member of the Coast Salish tribe who was visiting Victoria from his home near where Nanaimo now stands pointed out that plenty of the same stuff littered the riverbanks where he came from. In 1851, canoes carrying Hudson's Bay officials ran up to take a look and found the rich coal deposits of Nanaimo and New-castle Island. Marvelous! Their dependence on infrequent shipments of coal from England was no longer necessary. Local Indians willingly helped work the new mine in exchange for goods from Victoria. Unfortunately, the Haidas and other warlike tribes from the more northerly islands tended to raid southward at regular intervals. These raids caused the Hudson's Bay Company, in 1853, to construct its small but effective blockhouse, which could be used as a fortified shelter by the local population. Through the years the Bastion became an office, a store, even a local jail. And for a long period its cannon boomed out a ceremonial welcome for distinguished visitors arriving by sea in Nanaimo. Today the building is a small museum, well worth visiting, with artifacts from the days when the Bastion was the only military installation in the district.

It apparently served its purpose of protecting Nanaimo's infant industry, because the coal-mining venture was so successful that the town's second popular name is the City of Coal.

Just south of Nanaimo—about a mile's walk along busy Island Highway—is Petroglyph Park, the site of prehistoric carvings in solid rock outcroppings. The exact meaning of the carvings is not clear; they are mostly representations of human and animal forms, deeply carved or scratched into native rock. These mysterious figures probably date back to inhabitants who preceded the Coast Salish Indians of historic times.

These days, the biggest event of the year on Nanaimo's water-front is the annual Bathtub Race to Vancouver, held in July. All kinds of crazy, home-built small craft—some still actually constructed around old bathtubs and rigged with Rube Goldberg arrangements for power and steering—participate in this lighthearted event. They set out across the Strait of Georgia, adequately convoyed by more conventional vessels, and receive a tremendous welcome as they reach Vancouver. Visit Nanaimo in July and maybe you will be lucky enough to observe this singular marine event.

When the tidal currents are right for your departure, you will be ready to embark on Cruise Eight. But the departure point, you note, is Departure Bay. That is because it would be a shame to visit Nanaimo and fail to run through Newcastle Island Passage. Narrow and shallow, but well marked, this slim channel presents you on one side with a city waterfront that features the following highlights from south to north out of Commercial Inlet: the seaplane wharf; the Nanaimo Yacht Club floats; half a dozen privately operated marinas, only some of which offer transient moorage; and finally, just before you reach the big ferry docks, Brechin Boat Ramp, a new launch and haul-out incline with a large paved parking space for boat trailers. On the other side is a wooded park, untouched by commerce. Cruise Eleven tells you more about this park.

Beyond Pimbury and Shaft points you enter Departure Bay, and now your course swings east in a wide curve that circles halfway around Newcastle Island. As soon as you have a clear view up the middle of Northumberland Channel, you will set a course in that direction, keeping a watch out for the various kinds of water- and airborne-traffic that crisscross the surface of Nanaimo's extended harbor.

Do not edge very close to the southwestern shore of Northumberland Channel until you are well past the great Harmac timber processing plant. But once clear of it, you will want to bear to starboard and watch for the opening into Dodd Narrows. Even at slack, there can be substantial swirling of the water here. Often you will find a wide, racing whirlpool, easy enough to cut through with a little extra burst of speed in a powerboat, but something to expect and plan for if you are under sail.

Just to reinforce our comments about the state of Dodd Narrows at flood, or ebb, here are the words of a Canadian skipper out of Vancouver: "We've come through that pass a hundred times. Never had any trouble at or near slack water. But one time we took our boat through against the current at flood. She pulled and heeled a bit. On the other side, going fifteen knots, we stood still! That current was making fifteen knots against us! I had the power to double our speed, so we pulled away easily, but what if we'd had a displacement hull with a twelve knot maximum? We'd have been washed right back through the narrows."

On our own first passage of Dodd Narrows we arrived well in advance of ebb and went with the current, feeling the lift of a substantial following sea. It was magnificent: like two minutes on a rapid river, with reverse currents chuckling against the cliff-high banks. So it is possible to enter with confidence and enjoy an unusual two-minute experience. But be prepared by knowing what to expect of the narrows. The safest time for transit is *at slack water.*

South of this slim portal you run into the rapidly widening waters of Stuart Channel, with Mudge Island falling away from you to port and a long shore of Vancouver Island retreating to starboard. Take Round Island to starboard now, and make for the shore of De Courcy Island.

Without being sure what hour of the day you would reach this point, we planned an early stop for the night. Your destination now is Pirates Cove on the southeast corner of De Courcy Island, and you will reach it in less than an hour, even if you slow almost to a stop while enjoying the headlands and coves and tiny islands of Ruxton Passage. After entering Pylades Channel—at a point not far from your position two days ago—you have only to round the tip of De Courcy to port and you will come to Pirates Cove Marine Park.

This very special park is almost invisible from Pylades Channel. Even when you are quite close, a seaward projection covered with dense woods hides most of the sheltered basin that lies behind it. The primary landmark is a long rock reef. Be warned that it is far longer than it looks from your boat. Even at low water the reef continues below the surface in a straight line that stretches northwestward the length of a football field beyond its visible tip. The Parks Branch has established a natural range that enables skippers to negotiate this reef without trouble: a rock and a tree on the shore are both marked with white paint, and when you have the two aligned, you are properly positioned to enter the passage that leads between reef and shore into Pirates Cove.

Those familiar with the parallel ridges of rock that form both mountains and reefs in the Gulf Islands will not be surprised to discover that another broad reef bisects this entrance channel. Visible at low tide, this second reef lurks beneath the surface the rest of the time. The best course, in or out, is east of the channel's center, near the outer reef.

Pirates Cove is a large, excellent anchorage stretching well down toward the southernmost tip of De Courcy Island. It contains no moorage except two small, twelve-sided floats meant to accommodate dinghies. Too near the shore for larger vessels to approach safely, these floats give access to the park and the nine campsites available for the use of boatmen who carry tents. If the anchorage inside Pirates

Cove is crowded, as it may be on summer weekends, the indented shore of De Courcy Island just north of the entrance channel provides good alternate space.

A well has been drilled in the park and there are toilet facilities. Otherwise the immense beauty of the natural setting is undisturbed. Ashore, you can walk close to the water, enjoying a handsome view of the broken shoreline, or along a small road that links this sheltered spot with another at the north end of De Courcy. From there, you can explore the southwestern side of the island, which once witnessed some colorful experiments in colonization—largely because it was isolated from Vancouver Island and the mainland and therefore not regulated by mainstream society's rules.

A curious communelike settlement materialized here in the 1930s, and it must have been considered startlingly avant-garde in those days. All the women of the community, together with the group's "prophet," known as Brother Twelve, lived at the southern end of the island. All the other men lived at the northern end. De Courcy Island today has few buildings, and most of them are the remains of several forts that Brother Twelve built to protect his community from inquisitive visitors. From them, guns were fired to discourage trespassers.

Morning in a small marine park, many miles from the nearest settled community, is a marvelous experience. It may persuade you to stay an extra day in this delicate Eden. But Cruise Eight moves on.

You emerge from Pirates Cove back into Pylades Channel, a channel that is beginning to seem very familiar. Before heading south toward Trincomali, take a quick look around and read the names on your chart. Spain, nature, and the British navy share honors here, not always with careful attention to linguistic accuracy. "Gabriola," for example, is derived from *gaviota,* Spanish for sea gull. *Dibuxante* Josef Cordero was a draftsman aboard the *Mexicana,* and the name "Dibuxante Point" seems to commemorate his skill. Pylades Channel reminds us of the twenty-one-gun Royal Navy vessel H.M.S. *Pylades,* which was on station in this area from 1859 to 1861 and from 1869 to 1871.

Instead of spending the rest of the morning running the length of Trincomali Channel, we suggest you alter course to the west after rounding Pylades Island. Taking the beautifully austere Tree Island to starboard, you can examine its outlines from various angles, comparing it, perhaps, to a Japanese brush painting. Next, taking Danger Reefs to starboard, you can look northwest to the notch of Dodd Narrows and recall its glistening shores and chuckling currents. That notch, like a gaping tooth, is visible as far down Trincomali as Mon-

Vesuvius Bay near Salt Spring Island

tague Harbour, and if you noticed it on Cruise Six, you may have identified it then. Here, substantially closer, it draws your eye like a splash of color or an extra-tall sail.

Running well north of the reef that stretches out from Pilkey Point on Thetis Island, you now cross Stuart Channel to Yellow Point, which is located at the outermost limit of Ladysmith's extended harbor. This is a lovely spot, with handsome, long-distance marine views in every direction. It makes an excellent lunch stop, especially if you tie to the float or mooring buoys of the new Inn of the Sea and take your meal ashore in their gourmet dining room. The inn offers full hotel services, including a swimming pool. But we have seen many people in years past swimming in the unusually warm seawater that is found off the shore where the inn is now located.

After lunch you start out on the long run to Roche Harbor. It is quite a distance, and unless you are rushed, you may want to stop one more night en route. There are several possibilities. Because Cruise Eight from this point on directs you through familiar waters, we will not take space to describe again the passage of Sansum Narrows and Satellite Channel. We will not apologize for planning the return cruise over ground already covered, either, because Sansum Narrows is grand enough for many repeat visits. A night stop might be made by anchoring at Vesuvius, in the headwaters of Vesuvius Bay, with the majestic, tall reef to the south making stark silhouettes against the evening sky. Or, once you have cleared Separation Point, you might turn aside into the small marina in Genoa Bay, off Vancouver Island's

Cowichan Bay. Genoa Bay Marina is a friendly place with well-protected moorage, a pleasant little café, a small grocery store, showers, and campsites.

If you decide on one of these overnight stops, we urge you to visit Portland Island next morning on your way back to the San Juans. The entire island is a marine park named for Princess Margaret. It is undeveloped at present, but the Parks Branch has plans to provide a few amenities in the next several years. From Satellite Channel pass north of Piers Island, head eastward to the top of Shute Passage and then you have a choice of approaches. You may cross Shute Passage, run up the northwestern shore of Portland Island, go out and around Chads Islet and then into the small cove on the north end of the island. Anchorage here is good. Or you may turn down Shute Passage, go out and around Celia Reefs and Hood Islet southwest of Portland Island, then turn toward the island and run into the little bay

Vesuvius Store on Vesuvius Bay

on the south end of the island, setting your course between Hood and the Tortoise islets. Anchorage here is good except when a strong southeasterly is blowing. Dinghy ashore and take a leg-stretching walk up into the island's center, or stroll along its white, sandy beaches. Chances are good that you will have the park all to yourself. Even though Portland Island is situated on one of the busy sea traffic lanes of the region, pleasure boatmen have apparently not discovered its jewellike beauty.

From Portland Island your course will lie past Moresby Island, through Prevost Passage, and across Haro Strait to Turn Point where you head south to Roche Harbor and U.S. customs. From here any number of possible routes back to Anacortes are open to you, each of them covered in an earlier cruise. The choice is now up to you.

Cities, Parks, and Reflections from the Past

Cruises Nine through Twelve are individual, separate excursions. They are not linked, as Cruises One through Eight are linked, in a chain. Each represents a different approach to the islands, one you might take in place of the slower, linked cruises.

Cruises Nine and Ten are proffered to the pressed-for-time skipper who wants a rapid overview of the San Juan and Gulf islands, without meanders or lengthy explorations ashore. They are also designed to satisfy that certain breed of skipper, familiar in the Northwest, who simply enjoys being afloat and moving; who prefers the passing parade of boats and islands and sun and clouds to any harbor, however charming it may be; who delights in salt air, the wind, the occasional friendly porpoise or gull or leaping fish; who merely wants to go.

Possible stops and night moorages along the way are listed, and nautical miles estimated, but the number of days spent on each cruise will depend very much on your preferred or potential speed and on your inclination to investigate attractive spots ashore. So we will not attempt to give you specific duration figures.

Cruise Eleven stops only at small marine parks. It prompts us to appreciate the voters who support public recreation areas and to applaud those state and provincial officials who preserve the natural grace of our wooded wildernesses while taming them enough to supply campsites and moorages for our convenience. The parks we mention are accessible only by water or air; most of them are not very well known. They are treasured by all Northwest boating enthusiasts who have found them, but seaplanes are still rare in these quiet coves.

Cruise Twelve can be long or short. It traces the routes of the first European explorers who charted these border boating waters. Operating from a base in Nootka Sound on the western face of Vancouver Island, they produced these chartings in the summers of 1790 and 1791.

You can travel with Manuel Quimper and Juan Carrasco, viewing the maze of islands from the south—wondering at, but not sailing up the channels that frame and penetrate them. Or you can circumnavigate the San Juans, in two cruise segments, and in a third, explore the outer rim of the Gulf Islands, following José Narvaez and Juan Pantoja.

For this final cruise, you must carry along your own time machine.

Cruise
Nine

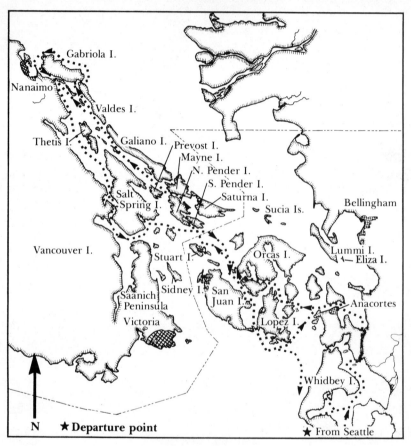

N   ★ Departure point
★ From Seattle

Do not use for navigation.
Use NOAA 18423, Folio Small-Craft Chart, and Canadian Hydrographic
Service Small Craft Chart 3310

Seattle to Nanaimo

Point of departure: Shilshole Bay, Puget Sound

Course: via Puget Sound, Possession Sound, Saratoga Passage, Skagit Bay, Swinomish Channel, Guemes Channel, Rosario Strait, Harney Channel, San Juan Channel, Haro Strait, Bedwell Harbour, Plumper Sound, Trincomali Channel, Dodd Narrows; return via Dodd Narrows, Stuart Channel, Sansum Narrows, Satellite Channel, Haro Strait, San Juan Channel, Middle Channel, Admiralty Inlet

Possible stops, brief or overnight: Langley, Coupeville, Oak Harbor, La Conner, Anacortes, James Island, Blind Island, Jones Island, Prevost Harbor, Bedwell Harbour (an essential stop for Canadian customs), Montague Harbour, Pirates Cove, Nanaimo, Telegraph Harbour, Maple Bay, Fulford Harbour, Friday Harbor (an essential stop for U.S. customs), Port Townsend, Everett Harbor

Length of cruise: approximately 135 nautical miles to Nanaimo; 270 nautical miles round trip

Threading the Archipelago

Seattle's Shilshole Bay Marina is a familiar spot to all Northwest boatmen, and vast numbers of pleasure-craft cruises originate behind the long stone breakwater of this enormous municipal facility. Cruise Nine starts here, leaving from Shilshole to head north up Puget Sound.

Our course is plotted to avoid the Vessel Traffic Lanes and to leave by the straightest way the congested waters near Seattle's commercial wharves. So, after rounding Meadow Point, you have only to cruise steadily north past Edwards Point, then a little east of north up Possession Sound, paralleling the eastern shoreline.

Because your purpose is to get to the islands as quickly as possible, you will not wish to put into the harbors of Edmonds or Everett. We suggest that you cross to the west side of Possession Sound just south of the Mukilteo ferry crossing and run north along the eastern shore of Whidbey Island. This long, triple-jointed island, which on the charts looks like an arthritic sea horse, will remain on your port hand for a considerable distance: until you enter Swinomish Channel.

Near Sandy Point, where Saratoga Passage pours into Possession Sound from the northwest, a pod of killer whales enlivened our last cruise through these waters. We cannot promise they will be there for you, however, since they cruise rapidly and widely through all of these inland waters. Their glistening black and white bodies arching out of the water in a series of great leaps will cause any skipper to throttle down and drift in their wake, amazed.

From Sandy Point your course lies northwestward up Saratoga Passage, first along the Whidbey Island shore, then across the passage to Lowell Point on Camano Island. If you are finding this run too long, or perhaps too choppy, a small municipal wharf at Langley will provide a leg-stretching stop. Other possible stops are farther north at Coupeville and Oak Harbor. Both require at least an hour's detour from your course, so unless you must have fuel (available at Oak Harbor) or can stay long enough to enjoy the lighthearted, well-executed restoration projects along the waterfront main street of Coupeville, it may be just as well to save these two harbors for another day.

Point Partridge on Whidbey Island

If you *can* stop at Coupeville, you will enjoy the camaraderie at the old floats. Large enough to hold about ten pleasure boats and linked by a picturesque warehouse to a long pier that juts out from the land, they wallow a bit in boat wash but afford access to a wholly charming village of several hundred relaxed souls. Here is a suggestion for you: read all the small signs you can find. One, fixed to the warehouse bulletin board at the head of the float-ramp, is protected by glass and gives directions for finding the harbor master. You first seek him in the office on the pier. If he is not there, you go up the main street to his home; then, "If no one at this location, go to Candle Factory. If no one at this location shout 'where's Wieringer' until the harbormaster appears or until you are arrested."

Resisting this entertaining detour, the uninterrupted Cruise Nine proceeds along the western shore of Camano Island, crosses into Skagit Bay on a diagonal from Rocky Point on Camano to Strawberry Point on Whidbey, and coasts northwestward toward the line of beacons that marks the Swinomish cut. This is a well-traveled route. You will have no difficulty discovering where to go because a variety of pleasure craft will keep you company all the way. Dangerous shallows in Skagit Bay are far enough to starboard to pose no problem if you stay reasonably close to Whidbey Island.

The Swinomish Channel feeds out of Skagit Bay at a right angle to your present course. Many people take one look at the chart and refuse to try this narrow canal unless an old-timer shepherds them through the first time—and that, of course, is a good way to go. However, the channel markers are very clear, and you can run the Swinomish alone the first time provided you take it slowly and pay attention to all the navigational aids marked on the chart. You turn east after lining up with the lighted range to the west of you in Dugualla Bay. Keeping even-numbered channel markers (nun buoys 2, 4, 6, 8) to starboard and bearing to starboard in the channel so that approaching vessels can pass close aside to your port, you make your way to the Hole in the Wall, an abrupt cut between bluffs opening northward. Soon a soaring orange bridge appears, spanning the high-walled channel. Passing beneath it you come to the fine little town of La Conner, which is spread like a checked cloth along the eastern bank of the Swinomish. Here the ground drops to flatlands, an extension of the rich Skagit Delta.

A stop at La Conner offers good dining at several excellent restaurants. Also, the town is a haven for artists and handcraftmen, whose products are available in a number of attractive shops decorated in the motifs of the 1890s. There are gas docks and two guest piers in the nearby Port of Skagit County marina. This recently enlarged facility is one of the best public marinas in the Northwest. It offers excellent launch facilities, showers, laundry, and marine repair. Nearby are markets, shore accommodations, and a fine museum on a hill overlooking La Conner's waterfront.

Leaving La Conner you push on northward, continuing through the Swinomish Channel and passing at its northern end beneath two more highway bridges and a swing-span railroad bridge. If you are cruising in a sailboat, one of the highway bridges will be lifted for you. The other rises from flatland and curves high overhead in a truly remarkable display of concrete spans and support pillars.

As you leave the Swinomish, your channel through Padilla Bay's shallows is also well marked. Keep your chart in hand and note the numbers on the day beacons as you pass, in order to see how far you have come. Rounding the long commercial piers off March Point, you approach Anacortes through the Capsante Waterway.

From Anacortes, you head west through Guemes Channel and across Rosario Strait to Thatcher Pass, enter the inner San Juan Is-

La Conner on the Swinomish Channel

lands between Decatur and Blakely islands, and alter course to the northwest (see Cruise One). Beyond Upright Head on Lopez Island, you run westward through the delightful narrows and bays of Harney Channel, reversing the last leg of Cruise Four. This time, however, you can turn away from Pole Pass, the thin, challenging portal between Crane and Orcas islands, and run out into San Juan Channel through Wasp Passage.

After this easier exit from Harney Channel, if the weather is good and the water reasonably placid, turn north and take Jones Island to port. Now head northwestward through open water toward Stuart Island, taking Flattop Island to port and then coasting along the northern shore of Stuart Island until you are opposite Bedwell Harbour on South Pender Island, across Haro Strait.

The cruise thus far has taken you through the middle of the San Juan Islands, with no detours or zigzags. You have been able to see and identify most of the major landfalls without trying to guess at the low-low-water locations of the seven-hundred-odd islands, islets, and rocks that are identified by geologists. In addition to Decatur, James, and Blakely, you have seen the widest stretch of Shaw Island, the distinctive promontories of Lopez, the beautiful, much-indented shore of Orcas, little Crane, the even smaller Wasp Islands, the well-loved marine park of Jones, and parts of San Juan, Spieden, and Stuart islands. Now, possibly after a stop at commodious, well-sheltered Prevost Harbor on Stuart, you cross over into Canada, on a northerly course (see Cruise Three).

The Canadian customs station is at Bedwell Harbour, so—after securing clearance—you may as well run up the harbor, through the delightful narrows of Shark Cove, and emerge into Port Browning (see Cruise Five). You are now well launched into the interior channels separating the northern Gulf Islands. Only a short distance away down Port Browning, you will join the primary inner artery that runs northwestward from Haro Strait almost to Nanaimo. Composed of Plumper Sound, Navy Channel, and Trincomali Channel, it will carry you to the doorstep of Nanaimo on Vancouver Island. However, one small ridge of land lies in the way. You can finish the outbound leg of your cruise either by going around this ridge through Gabriola Passage or by cutting through it at Dodd Narrows, each of which is a splendidly scenic avenue (see Cruises Seven and Eight). And so you come at last, through McKay Channel, to the City of Coal, Bastion City, Nanaimo.

Nanaimo is the depot for pleasure craft that plan to head on northward into the fjord-laced British Columbia coastal waters, Desolation Sound, the Queen Charlotte Islands, and eventually, Alaska. *Border Boating* stops at Nanaimo, which is widely held to be the keystone of the Gulf Islands. From this point you will head back south to Seattle. However, because the charms of Nanaimo are many, you should stay long enough to explore the city if you can spare the time (see Cruise Eight). It blends tribal heritage and coal wealth, current commerce with the city of Vancouver and roots stretching back to the Hudson's Bay Company. From the harbor it is a beautiful sight, spread in blocks and squares of color over the green hills.

The homeward course from Nanaimo duplicates that of Cruise Eight, but returns to Bedwell Harbour by way of Satellite Channel. From Bedwell you are urged to retrace your present cruise's path as far as the Wasp Islands and, from there, to proceed down San Juan Channel to Friday Harbor, the U.S. customs station.

From Friday Harbor you can cruise around little Turn Island, head south for Middle Channel, and then return up Rosario Strait to Anacortes, the Swinomish, Saratoga Passage, and Shilshole Bay (see Cruise One). Or, if the day is shining and beckons you to open waters, you can return to your departure point by coasting along the outside (western) shore of Whidbey Island, entering Puget Sound as Captain George Vancouver first did and as freighters do today, through Admiralty Inlet.

One concept you might like to keep in mind while following Cruise Nine is this: you are passing on a rough diagonal up some two thirds of the great inland sea whose tidal waters pour in and out through the Strait of Juan de Fuca. Yet, with the briefest of exceptions, you do not find yourself exposed to the larger channels of this inland sea. There are, in other words, numerous *inner* inland channels—each protected by Gulf or San Juan islands as well as by Vancouver Island and the mainland. One of these lies inside Whidbey Island, another lies inside the broken barrier of Saturna, Galiano, Valdes, and Gabriola islands, and a third cuts through the center of the San Juan Islands. This conformation of land and waters is what makes border boating possible to small boats and magnificently comfortable for all pleasure craft.

Cruise
Ten

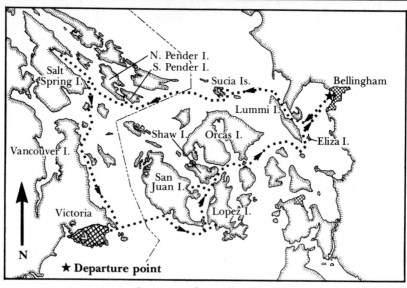

Do not use for navigation.
Use NOAA 18423, Folio Small-Craft Chart, and Canadian Hydrographic
Service Small Craft Chart 3310

Bellingham, Ganges, and Victoria

Point of departure: Bellingham

Course: via Bellingham Bay, Hale Passage, Strait of Georgia, Boundary Pass, Haro Strait, Bedwell Harbour, Swanson Channel, Ganges Harbour, Moresby Passage, Bazan Bay, Cordova Channel, Baynes Channel, Oak Bay; return via Haro Strait, Middle Channel, San Juan Channel, Upright Channel, East Sound, Peavine Pass, Rosario Strait, Bellingham Bay

Possible stops, brief or overnight: Fossil Bay on the Sucia Islands, Bedwell Harbour (an essential stop for Canadian customs), Ganges, Portland Island, Oak Bay, Friday Harbor (an essential stop for U.S. customs)

Length of cruise: approximately 128 nautical miles round trip

Triangle to the Sun

The purpose of Cruise Ten is to outline a course that departs from a point midway between the two sets of border islands rather than from Anacortes. Bellingham, on the mainland some seventeen miles south of the Canadian border, lies approximately on a line with Satellite Channel and with that part of Haro Strait that separates the Gulf Islands from the San Juan Islands. This cruise has two outbound destinations that reflect and encompass western Canadian development: Ganges, on Salt Spring Island, and Victoria, which dominates Vancouver Island, the vast landmass that shields the border islands from the Pacific Ocean. It focuses on those Gulf Islands that face on Haro Strait, and it returns through one of the inner San Juan channels. It gives you a substantial sampling of the border region. And if it does not provide a full survey, remember that we hope you will come back for a closer look another day.

In Bellingham, a small city that is pushing toward a population of fifty thousand, you will find Squalicum Harbor, a good-sized municipal marina or boat haven named after Squalicum Creek, which pours into the bay beside it. Guest moorage—for those who arrive in Bellingham by water—is located close to the innermost Squalicum docks.

However, those who trailer their boats to Bellingham will want to drive to the parking area and launch ramp at the southern terminal of the port. Located near the foot of Harris Street in Old Fairhaven Village, on the south side of town, this facility is well marked and easy to locate.

As you set out southwestward down Bellingham Bay, heading for Point Frances, be sure to look back at the town. With its small high-rise center clustering in a fold between Sehome Hill to the south and a tall, level bluff to the north, Bellingham pours residential structures over all the foothills in sight, dividing them with streets that appear to rise vertically from the water, streets that lie so truly east-west that compasses are corrected by reference to them. Travelers like to debate whether this sea view reminds them more of a Mediterranean city or of a town on the coast of Norway.

Behind the city, like an unbelievably theatrical backdrop, rises the brilliant cone of Mount Baker, capped with its permanent snows. As

Regatta in Bellingham Bay

you might guess from the sight of this mountain, Bellinghamites who somehow escape the lure of the islands are devotees of the ski slopes instead.

Rounding Point Frances, you cruise to the northwest up the short, serene narrows of Hale Passage, where—wonder of wonders—the Lummi Island ferry is likely to throttle down for you if you approach on its starboard quarter (see Cruise Four). When you are abeam of Migley Light, you will be entering the ill-defined confluence of Georgia and Rosario straits. Crossing this stretch of open water on a westerly heading, you will want to stay alert for deep-draft vessels, tugs-and-tows, and tankers heading for Cherry Point or the harbor of Vancouver. Wakes and bow waves from any of these heavy hulls are likely to create a real upheaval of waters for small craft.

Your immediate goal is Fossil Bay on the Sucia Islands. (This long, narrow harbor was briefly described in Cruise Five.) Most popular, hence most crowded, of the four major havens in Sucia Islands State Park, Fossil Bay also has several weighty claims to the title of "most beautiful moorage in the islands." Its double row of mooring buoys runs down the center of the harbor, lined up fortuitously with a notch in the island into which the westering sun drops like a bird settling into its nest. As a result, narrow ribbons of golden fire streak down Fossil Bay at sunset; its headwaters and shoreline turn crimson; its rim of rigid evergreens stands out in sharp black silhouette against the incredible brilliance of the western sky. Campers walking the cliff path or standing awestruck near their tents are one-dimensional and

Fossil Bay on Sucia Island

black, like the trees, and motionless, as if arrested at the door of an open furnace. To one side a great, bare sandstone cliff, sister to the one in Shallow Bay (see Cruise Five), crowds the floats, picking up reflected color. Hikers along its crest are small and silent as toys.

Is it fair to other lovely spots that Fossil Bay should also capture a dazzling picture eastward at daybreak? In the distance you see Barnes and Clark islands, lying low to the water, and the soaring shape of

Lummi Island beyond. Fog often hugs the waterline of Lummi like a feather boa and lifts, thinning, to burn off under the midmorning sun.

If you have the time, walk along the foreshore below the high cliff on the narrow south side of Sucia, outside Fossil Bay. Here the rocks contain abundant fossils of life dating back to the Cretaceous period of sixty million or more years ago.

As you depart from Fossil Bay, swing south along this same shore. Allow ample room for the rock shelf that reaches far out into the water, invisible except at low tide. Sucia means "foul," remember. These are the waters that the Spanish explorers found to be hazardous to their wooden-keeled, displacement-hulled vessels.

Your course now lies west across Boundary Pass to the southern faces of Saturna and the Penders. You will clear customs at Bedwell Harbour, emerge again into Haro Strait, and follow the shore of North Pender Island up vigorous Swanson Channel (see Cruise Five). We always encounter chop here. All other waters may occasionally lie flat as a pond, but Swanson Channel seems always to be deeply textured and pulled by conflicting currents.

You cross from Mouat Point to Beaver Point on Salt Spring Island and run through increasingly protected waters into the municipal harbor at Ganges (see Cruise Seven). This charming town, with its aura of historic importance, surely warrants a stopover, however brief. It can also replenish ship's stores, supply fuel, provide reading materials, chandlery items, and marine repairs. Its panoramic view southward of overlapping island forms is enticing and pulls at your cruising appetite like a magnet. From the high mass of Salt Spring's own uplift to the Penders and distant Stuart Island, you see paler and paler shades of deep blue and purple with wide shining paths of water between.

Leaving Ganges, you head southwestward and then south to pass between Portland and Moresby islands. If you wish to linger a bit longer in these waters, consider a stop at Portland Island, all of which constitutes the Princess Margaret Marine Park (see Cruise Eight). The island was given to Princess Margaret by the people of British Columbia in 1958. But the princess returned it to the province nine years later so that it could be added to the growing provincial marine park system.

Weaving cautiously among the small fringe islands clustering near Saanich Peninsula, you will emerge at last into the relatively open waters of Bazan Bay and Cordova Channel (see Cruise Three). In fact, these waters may be more open than you would like, because they border on Haro Strait. Keep near Vancouver Island—avoiding shoals marked on your chart—and you will escape much of the chop.

Soon after entering Baynes Channel, you will find yourself inside rock-strewn Oak Bay, the location of our preferred moorage for the city of Victoria. Oak Bay Marina, approached by a well-marked channel, offers all the supplies and amenities you might need, except groceries and shore accommodations, and both of these are available nearby. By putting in at Oak Bay you avoid the rocky shores and congested approaches to Victoria's inner harbor. Reservations, of course, are desirable.

Victoria is a gem. If you have not already made its acquaintance by car and ferry, you should certainly do so now. At Oak Bay itself is Sealand, an oceanarium that features a show by trained seals, sea lions, and a killer whale. A municipal bus runs regularly near Oak Bay Marina, and after some twenty minutes it deposits you close to the promenade embankment that overlooks Victoria Harbour. Here the tall, old Empress, westernmost of those grand railroad hotels that lie across Canada like a string of elegant beads, dominates the embankment on one side, while the Parliament Buildings stretch along another in a frame of well-kept lawns. The famous green copper roofs of these two structures shine overhead, and baskets of blossoming flowers hang from every streetlight. At night, rows of lights outline the Parliament Buildings, reflecting vividly in the water of the harbor. Distinctive shopping areas with a British flavor, restored historic sights, a superb museum, many restaurants, and other attractions for visitors make this city remarkably appealing. Afternoon tea with crumpets or muffins in the lobby of the Empress, or a glass of shooting sherry in the hotel's licensed lounge, will evoke the spirit of Queen Victoria's imperial glory.

Your return route takes you directly across Haro Strait near its mouth, unless the small-craft advisories are flying on the day you propose to leave Oak Bay. If it is very windy, a heavy chop may oblige you to run north instead, in the lee of the big island, crossing Haro near Turn Point on Stuart Island. But if you have a reasonable day, make directly for the nearest point on San Juan Island's southwestern face (see Cruise Twelve). Run southeastward along the San Juan coast toward rocky, weather-beaten Cattle Point, with its bare rock supporting a handsome lighthouse. Clear the point and alter course northward up Middle Channel. Your customs stop will be Friday Harbor, just after you round Turn Island at the bend in San Juan Channel. After clearance you leave the harbor, pass Turn Island once again, and traverse Upright Channel (see Cruise Two). Then cross the southern waters of East Sound, thread through the slim, attractive cut of Peavine Pass, and emerge into Rosario Strait.

Having earlier crossed the undoubtedly rolling waters at the mouth of Haro Strait, you will be undaunted by the somewhat open passage that stretches away north and south at this point. So you will push on to cross Rosario Strait on a northeasterly course, passing wide around the north shore of Sinclair Island to run between Viti Rocks and Lummi Island.

Glance up, for a moment, at the steep face of Lummi Peak and notice the long, barren slides that plunge down the mountainside into the sea. These are known collectively as the Devil's Rock Slide; fatal accidents have befallen climbers who have attempted to scale the slides, have lost their footing in the loose, gravelly surface, and have plunged, together with sliding pebbles and boulders, into the sea below.

The shortest route back to your departure point now lies between graceful little Eliza Island and Lummi. In fact, as you turn into this channel you can begin to see, some seven miles away, factory smokestacks, church spires, and an indistinct wash of buildings that mark Bellingham, the end of your journey. Only a quick run across the bay remains. How many days were you out? Three? Four? Seven?

Cruise
Eleven

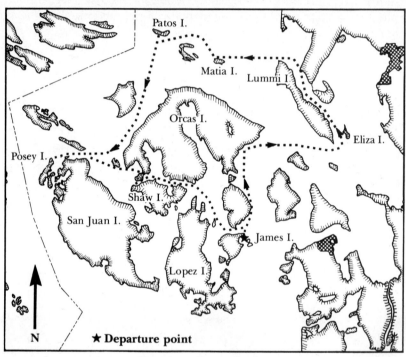

Do not use for navigation.
Use NOAA 18423, Folio Small-Craft Chart

From James to Patos to Posey

Point of departure: James Island, San Juan County

Course: via Rosario Strait to Doe Island; via Rosario Strait, Hale Passage and Strait of Georgia to Lummi Island Camp and Picnic Area and Matia and Patos islands; via President, San Juan, and Spieden channels to Posey Island; return course optional

Stops, brief or overnight: James Island, Doe Island, Lummi Island Camp and Picnic Area, Matia Island, Patos Island, Posey Island

Length of cruise: approximately 49 nautical miles from James Island to Posey Island

Duration on power from James to Posey: 3 to 4 days

Duration on sail from James to Posey: 4 to 6 days

A Salute to the Small Marine Parks

Many of the smaller marine parks in the San Juan Islands are almost unknown. In contrast to the Sucias and Jones and Prevost, they have been largely overlooked by cruising boatmen. Most are accessible only by water and offer few amenities, but they are free of charge and delightfully unspoiled. These smaller parks are varied, too. Some offer room for one or two vessels, others are not crowded by a dozen or more; some have fresh water, some are dry; some are too small for campsites but provide fire rings for barbecues ashore, others can screen half a dozen tents in their thickly forested coves.

Cruise Eleven makes no attempt to touch them all. If you like the ones we suggest, you can always look for others and pick your own favorites. For now we propose that you sample a series of six parks arranged roughly in a crescent northward and westward around the periphery of the major San Juan Islands.

Begin with James Island, which lies near Decatur Head at the mouth of Thatcher Pass (see Cruise One). James Island, consisting of two high, round hills connected by a narrow waist, is all park, 113 acres in extent. A rich forest of fir, cedar, and madrona covers it from shore to shore, and its campsites are shaded bowers full of woodland scents. The ground may be chilly and sometimes damp, but it is never dusty.

The shape of this island creates two sheltered coves, but each is subject, to some extent, to the tidal currents and winds of Rosario Strait. Most sheltered is the eastern cove, even though it faces directly onto the usually vigorous strait. The saddle between the hills rises gently from the western cove to about seventy-five feet at its crest. From the eastern cove it rises more abruptly. Here, jutting headlands of rock deflect the strait's stronger currents, and four mooring buoys dot the quiet water within. The only dock is on the western side, however, and dock moorage gives easy access to the island's high waist. The floats at the dock will accommodate about four twenty-six-foot boats, but rafting increases the number of craft usually found there in the summer season.

Just south of these floats, there is a solitary mooring buoy anchored in the center of a swiftly moving tidal current. One day we tied our boat *Sea Scribbler* to this buoy and watched apprehensively while the current tugged us hard enough to pull the buoy completely under water. Fortunately, it held. The bottom on the western side is not good for anchoring, however. While we watched our own mooring lines, two sailboat skippers tried to get their hooks to hold, failed, and went off around Decatur Head looking for other anchorage. A third skipper took a chance that his anchor would hold and woke up next morning on the rocks, shouting for help.

Ashore there are seven or eight campsites, barbecue pits, and one large fire ring surrounded by benches made of huge split logs resting in notched cross sections of log. Whatever else may change, these massive benches are bound to be here to welcome in the twenty-first century. The park has pit toilets and trash receptacles, but thus far it does not have fresh water, so bring your own drinking water with you.

Excellent trails have been cut to the hilltops of James Island, and the outlook, especially from the crest of South Hill, provides a striking panorama of Rosario Strait. The natural growth around the trails is undisturbed. Salal and wild currant grow between the boles of tall cedars and hemlock. Birds are plentiful, including bald eagles, belted kingfishers, and the ubiquitous northwestern crow.

Leaving James Island, you head north up Rosario Strait, keeping near the shore of Blakely Island. It would be wise to swing wide around the openings of Peavine and Obstruction passes, since sport-fishing boats cluster at these mouths like swarming bees. A short run up the shore of Orcas Island brings you to little Doe Island, another state marine park, nestled just offshore. The small dock that gives access to this park is located on the island's inner face, where there is some shelter from the southeasterlies that often course up Rosario Strait during our best boating seasons. In fall and winter, winds from the strait are so severe that the park authorities take up Doe Island's floats around the end of September and do not put them back in the water until around the end of April. This practice, also followed at James, Jones, and Matia islands and for the innermost float at Fossil Bay on Sucia, is a protective measure, to prevent the floats being broken up by winter storms. If you like the security of tying to floats, be sure to plan your parks cruise for sometime between the middle of May and the middle of September, when they are in place.

Doe Island Marine Park is a tiny jewel, about four acres in extent. There are several miniature beaches along the shoreline, connected by a trail that leads around the island. Five campsites, some trash containers, and a couple of pit toilets are the only "improvements." But sport fishermen often converge here, because the waters up and down this side of Orcas Island have a local reputation for providing abundant catches.

The little channel that separates Doe Island from Orcas Island is slender and graceful. Homes on the larger island make an attractive shore, and a few vessels moored to private buoys ride quietly in the sheltered water. As you explore this channel, be careful of the reef lying off the south shore of Doe Island; it has some wicked rock projections.

Leaving Doe Island, you cross Rosario Strait, heading northeastward for Carter Point on Lummi Island. After entering the channel that separates Lummi from Eliza Island, you should coast slowly up the eastern face of the former, watching for a sign mounted on a rock promontory. The sign reads "Lummi Island Camp and Picnic Area, Division of Natural Resources, State of Washington." These words may remind you that not all those areas commonly called state parks are owned or developed by the same governmental agency. Current government records list only six full-scale state parks within the San Juan archipelago, while there are an additional thirty-one designated islands and recreational sites in this area that are under the administration of the Washington State Parks and Recreational Commission. Other agencies engaged in the administration of public lands designated as parks include the Department of Natural Resources, as indicated above, and the Department of Fish and Wildlife. In addition, the Department of Game provides a good many boat ramps. To avoid unnecessary confusion, we have referred to all of the parks on Cruise Eleven as state parks, without trying to distinguish which agencies run them.

Behind the rocky promontory bearing the sign that identifies Lummi Island's park, there is a nick in the tall side of the island. In this world where there are so many of us that we crowd and jostle each other in parks from coast to coast, would you believe there is park that is not crowded and cannot ever get crowded? You are now looking at one. It is first come, first served in the waters below this park and second come, second served; but after that nothing much larger than a beachable day boat will be able to squeeze in. There are no mooring buoys or floats here. You must either anchor or beach, and since the anchorage is tiny and the beach very limited, three boats constitute a full house.

Accessible in theory by land and by sea, the campground is used by none but the hardiest hikers, who have pushed far enough down the side of Lummi's mountainous flank to discover it. Boats bring most of the visitors, who enjoy the modest amenities perched precariously on the layered, steep mountainside that constitutes this park.

Lummi Island Camp and Picnic Area

Fire pits and picnic areas face out over limpid blue channels to a breathtaking view of the mainland that includes the Canadian Coast Range, Mount Baker, and the shouldering hills of Chuckanut Mountain. Park amenities include a steep set of steps leading up from the pebbled beach that rims your minute harbor to a rather rugged, cliff-hugging trail that takes you to two additional tiny beaches, and several lookout points. Along the way you will find some picnic tables, toilets, and trash containers. Once again, bring your own water.

Lying at anchor between the high walls of this tiny inlet, watching gulls and hawks wheel overhead, and counting pebbles through the clear water below, you can be excused for suspecting you have finally discovered paradise.

From the Lummi Island park you proceed up Hale Passage to Migley Light, then alter course westward in order to cross the Strait of Georgia to Matia Island (see Cruise Four). This crossing is an open piece of water, given frequently to chop and rolling swells. But you can easily see your destination lying in dark, sharp outline just ahead.

Matia Island Marine Park often accommodates overflow from its near neighbor Echo Bay on the Sucia Islands; so in midsummer you can expect to find it crowded unless you arrive sometime in the morning. Its attractive harbor, nestled inside beautifully honeycombed, high, sandstone ridges, is protected from north, east, and south winds. Only the rather rare westerly disturbs it, and even in a westerly, Matia derives some protection from the wind-breaking cliffs of Sucia. Matia was used in a variety of ways before the whole island was finally set aside as a park. In the early years of the century it supported a fox farm, and in parts of the island agriculture was once tried. But these attempts at settlement have left few marks: some wooden and wire fences, a couple of tumbledown buildings, and an occasional clearing in the forest.

The trees on the island are old and tall, and the sheltered interior basin supplies excellent campsites, drinking water, and hiking trails that lead to secluded beaches. The one dock at Matia is small and there are few mooring buoys, but the bottom holds well on the westward-facing coves near the harbor. There is also room for eight or more anchored boats inside the harbor itself. Our one attempt to anchor in the southeastern cove was frustrated by very active water and masses of sea grasses; so we do not think of it as a desirable spot. But on tranquil summer days boats are often there. East of Matia is little Puffin Island, frequented by many kinds of water birds, including the tufted puffin, or sea parrot. The rocky stretch between these two islands is sometimes used for anchorage, too, although it is risky and we do not advise it.

The next stop on Cruise Eleven is at nearby Patos, another island park. Marking the U.S. side of Boundary Pass and holding title as the northernmost island in the San Juans, Patos is located just slightly northwest of Sucia. It is more exposed to wind and weather than the other islands on this cruise, with the consequence that greater care must be used in anchoring here. The southwest corner, between Patos and Little Patos Island, in Active Cove, offers the best shelter. The

Posey Island Marine Park

cove is entered from the west. There is a single mooring buoy here; if it is taken, anchorage should be made as close to it as possible, allowing for safe clearance of your boat in its swing. Do not tie up at the old Coast Guard dock, which is too exposed to wind and sea for comfort and safety. At Alden Point a handsome lighthouse warns of severe tide rips, whirlpools, and reefs. Relatively few visitors come to Patos, which has only recently been developed as a park, but you will find four campsites, sandy beaches, and excellent fishing near its shores. On warm summer days, boatmen enjoy picnicking on the grassy slopes of Patos, beachcombing along the shores, and exploring the many tide pools. Scuba divers often gather here to probe beneath the surface of the crystal-clear water.

Picnic tables, barbecue pits, trash receptacles, and pit toilets have been installed at Patos, but once again, drinking water is not available. The lack of heavy forest means that a considerable part of the island's twenty-four acres can be walked with ease.

No one lives in the lightkeeper's house these days, because the great light has been automated. Today Patos is cared for by the parks department crew that headquarters on Sucia Island.

From Patos your course lies south and southwest down President Channel until you reach Jones Island; from there you will cross San Juan Channel, thread Spieden Channel, and approach the entrance to Roche Harbor. Helping to shelter Roche Harbor is small, privately owned Pearl Island, a long, narrow landfall that has a number of good beaches lining its shore. Not surprisingly, this island supports many handsome homes. Off its northwestern tip lies tiny Posey Island Marine Park, a curious little one-acre patch of rock covered with scant shrubbery that displays many beautiful wild flowers in the spring. The pleasure of a visit to Posey is increased if you are a confirmed boat watcher. The adjacent channel into Roche Harbor provides a non-stop parade of pleasure craft, all sizes, all colors, and, unfortunately, all speeds. You can picnic on Posey and sit in bemused wonder as they pass: with silent grace or noisy engines, flying U.S. ensigns or the red mapleleaf, sprouting radio antennae and fishing poles, most of them responding readily to your waves.

You can anchor between Posey and Pearl islands and spend the night, or you may elect—after an hour or so—to head on home. If you stay, there are tables, fire rings, a single campsite, and an aged but usable pit toilet. When you decide to leave, the return route may be one of several already described in Cruises One through Ten. If you want to stick with parks, a course that links Posey, Jones, Blind, and James islands will take you quickly back to your departure point.

On Cruise Eleven we have plotted a course that includes only American marine parks, although Canada has established many similar facilities, both large and small, in the Gulf Islands. We reasoned that a sampling of parks on a short cruise would demonstrate the delights of these preserves, while a long cruise stopping exclusively at parks might prove monotonous. And distance makes a short cruise that includes both American and Canadian marine parks impossible.

Many of the most enjoyable Canadian marine parks have already been fully described in "Inner and Outer Islands of the Gulf": Beaumont Marine Park in Cruise Five, Montague Harbour Marine Park in Cruise Six, Pirates Cove Marine Park and Ganges waterfront park in Cruise Seven, and the undeveloped Princess Margaret Marine Park in Cruise Eight. You could plot a handsome cruise merely by stepping from one to another of these recreational preserves north of the border.

We cannot leave this subject, however, without a mention of the most distant but in some ways most appealing of the parks you might have occasion to visit while border boating. This is Newcastle Island Park in Nanaimo Harbour. Many skippers prefer to moor at the floats of Newcastle instead of at the boat basin of Nanaimo, convenient and attractive as the latter is, and make only a brief visit to the city for supplies. Newcastle Island is large and magnificently wooded, and has piped fresh water. There are eighteen camping units, and a small fretwork of floats is capable of mooring many boats. The water is cold, but enthusiasts find it pleasant for swimming. Until recently, a pedestrian ferry brought people here, and there is hope that it will resume service, but no cars are allowed. Trails and picnic accommodations provide pleasure to a great many visitors every year.

It may have occurred to you by now that a full survey of marine parks throughout the border islands would fill a good-sized book, a fact very much to the credit of public-spirited denizens of both Washington State and the Province of British Columbia. Hurray for us!

Cruise
Twelve

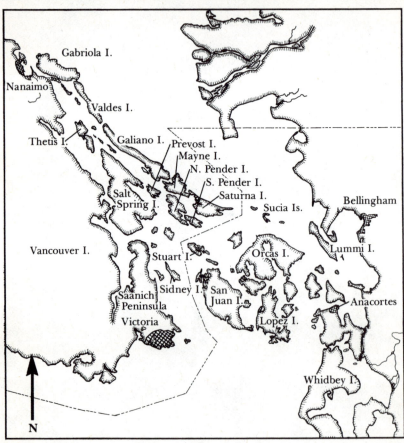

Gabriola I.

Nanaimo

Valdes I.

Thetis I.

Galiano I.

Prevost I.

Mayne I.

N. Pender I.

S. Pender I.

Salt
Spring I.

Saturna I.

Sucia Is.

Bellingham

Vancouver I.

Stuart I.

Orcas I.

Lummi I.

Sidney I.

San
Juan I.

Saanich
Peninsula

Anacortes

Victoria

Lopez I.

Whidbey I.

N

Do not use for navigation.
Use NOAA 18423, Folio Small-Craft Chart, and Canadian Hydrographic
Service Small Craft Chart 3310

In the Wake of the Spanish Explorers, 1790 and 1791

Point of departure: Race Rocks, near Victoria, British Columbia

Course: back and forth across the Strait of Juan de Fuca; north up Haro Strait; north up Rosario Strait

Length of cruise: variable; you will want to select the parts of it that appeal to you

Duration of cruise: also variable; it took the Spaniards the better part of two summers

The Sea of the West

For this cruise, you must activate your imagination. Put it into overdrive.

From the cockpit of your boat you are going to trace those first two summers of exploration, 1790 and 1791. You will follow the captains of Spain, Quimper and Eliza, as they or their lieutenants skippered the first European vessels through Juan de Fuca, Haro, and Rosario, and even into the Strait of Georgia. You will be striving to see with the Spaniards' eyes, of course, and to share their expectations. So you must also share their primary disappointments: one, that the inland waters of the Pacific Northwest were smaller than had been estimated, and two, that no Northwest Passage materialized.

To those of us who live beside these waters, it seems impossible that anyone could have considered our inland sea small. The very thought raises our hackles. But early charts, drawn mostly by guesswork, had depicted the "Sea of the West" as inundating an enormous area inside the opening they called Fuca. In 1752 this imaginary inland sea was charted as if it occupied half the area between Fuca and Hudson's Bay. And in 1782 it swelled into a huge balloon almost twenty times the size of nearby Lake Michigan.

In each of the early speculative charts, a broad water corridor— the coveted Northwest Passage—led conveniently from the Sea of the West to the Atlantic Ocean. It was the Spanish explorers' assignment to find that corridor, before men of other nations did so.

Like every other European mariner who probed the Strait of Juan de Fuca in the decade between 1790 and 1800, the Spanish commandants sought that imaginary Northwest Passage first and foremost, allowing all other merits of the inland sea to take second billing. In tracing their voyages, you will need to remember their consuming interest in channels that appeared to trend eastward. Then you can understand their failure to explore promising watercourses that opened in other directions.

The early Spaniards were career men, under orders to return with detailed navigational charts that other ship captains could easily follow. Fortunately, many of their charts have been preserved through the centuries, making it possible for us present-day skippers to follow along, envisioning primeval forests broken only by occasional fire scars, channels traversed by Indian dugout canoes, and masses of otters romping near inland shores.

A cruise plotted literally in the wake of these Spanish seamen makes an exciting, demanding excursion. Knowing what you already know of these waters, and with detailed NOAA charts to lead you every mile of the way, you will marvel at Quimper and Pantoja and Eliza and Narvaez, who felt their way slowly along unknown coasts— in fog, rain, and sun—spinning their charts behind them like cobwebs.

The two Spanish expeditions that are especially good to follow are the first, brief circling of 1790 and the long, detailed probing of 1791. Between them, they covered most of the waters through which we have plotted Cruises One to Eleven. The more famous 1792 explorations led English and Spanish vessels far south into Puget Sound and far north around Vancouver Island to the Pacific. But it was Quimper and Eliza who first focused on our border boating waters; hence it is Quimper and Eliza whom we follow in Cruise Twelve.

On 28 June 1790 the *Princesa Real,* under the command of Manuel Quimper, passed between Race Rocks and Bentinck Island off the coast of Vancouver Island, just to the west and south of the site of Victoria. She had coasted down from Nootka Sound on the west side of Vancouver Island and had sailed up the Strait of Juan de Fuca, charting its northern shoreline. A modest-sized sloop—forty-three feet long on her keel and sixteen feet wide at the beam—she drew between seven and a half and eight feet of water. Many of today's racing sailboats are as long and as broad as the *Princesa Real.* Some of our twin-screw flying-bridge cruisers have as much or more superstructure than the *Princesa Real,* although fully rigged she must have seemed a bulky shape to the Indians who watched her pass. The tribal war canoes could be easily as long as the forty-three-foot Spanish vessel, but they rose little higher than a log out of the water. Nor could the canoes carry as many people. Piloted by Gonzalo Lopez de Haro and Juan Carrasco, the *Princesa Real* carried her three officers, forty-one seamen, and nine soldiers. How many are there in your crew?

To follow Quimper's voyage, you should start in the waters between Race Rocks and Victoria. After exploring and naming the area immediately around today's provincial capital, Quimper sent second pilot Carrasco in the ship's longboat to explore farther around the south coast of Vancouver Island and beyond, to north and east. Carrasco's vessel, probably eighteen to twenty feet long, would have been fitted with one or two sets of oars and a mast that could be stepped when needed. In it, the pilot sighted the strait, which was promptly named for his immediate superior, first pilot Lopez de Haro. The

Cattle Point on San Juan Island

name has not disappeared with time.

From Baynes Channel, east of Victoria, you will be able to see what Carrasco saw: a wide waterway to the north and the Strait of Juan de Fuca broadening into an oval as it penetrates eastward. If you have a clear day, you will see the distant line of Whidbey Island, but Carrasco probably saw little more than vague outlines in the distance. Quimper's expedition suffered much bad weather, and when Carrasco saw Haro for the first time, fog lay in both straits, as it often does in June. He could easily see, however, the nearby shore of San Juan Island, and he named its nearest headland Punta Herrara (today's Bellevue Point).

Quimper's expedition pushed no farther north. Why did neither Carrasco nor Quimper himself explore more than the opening of Haro Strait? Apparently it was because the Indians in the Esquimalt area had assured Quimper in sign language that this channel trended northwestward. And it does. But the sought-after Northwest Passage would have to lie to the east in order to reach the Atlantic. Precious time would be lost if the expedition allowed itself to be lured off in the wrong direction.

On 4 July the weather finally improved, and the *Princesa Real* crossed from Esquimalt Harbour to the south side of Juan de Fuca. To follow, plot a course for Dungeness Spit, where the Spanish ship anchored that night. A few days later she sailed back again to Esquimalt Harbour to chart it in detail, and three days after that she crossed the strait once more, to inch along the Washington coast from

Freshwater Bay out to Neah Bay. Then she headed south down the Pacific rim to San Blas on the Mexican coast.

The above cruise, composed of several crossings of one of our most turbulent pieces of open water, may not inspire you to emulation. But the one-day longboat excursion that put out from the mother ship while she lay at Dungeness might be very attractive.

Again, it was pilot Carrasco who set forth, leaving Quimper to gather from the Indians what information he could about the Northwest Passage.

Carrasco explored the northern coasts of Miller and Quimper peninsulas without seeing Sequim Bay. You will perhaps be able to imagine how easily this beautiful, deep inlet could be missed. Carrasco reported the presence of Discovery Bay (also called Port Discovery on some charts), mentioning that it had plenty of fresh water for the depleted barrels aboard the *Princesa Real*; afterward he ran east until he could clearly see Point Wilson, which today shelters Port Townsend. If you reach this spot, you will perhaps guess at Carrasco's disappointment. Instead of an opening to the east, he saw an unbroken wall of land stretching north and south to the limits of sight. It completely closed off the end of the Strait of Juan de Fuca. An opening just ahead of him to starboard apparently led into another small bay, similar no doubt to Discovery Bay. But it was time to return with his report; so Carrasco named the bay Ensenada de Caamano and came about on his return course. He took careful note of a wide break in the shoreline to the north—an opening that looked well worth exploring. He also charted a small, easterly cut through the high wall that faced him, and a promontory that others to follow could easily identify. You know these three places as Rosario Strait, Deception Pass, and Point Partridge.

And there, still hovering off the coast of the Olympic Peninsula, almost but not quite within sight of Admiralty Inlet, we can leave Quimper's expedition. By zigzagging out of the Strait of Juan de Fuca, these first official explorers managed to miss Ediz Hook and the site of Port Angeles entirely.

Quimper's chart of his summer's explorations looks vaguely like a geoduck clam with its long neck thrust out to the ocean. Beyond the shoreline drawing, it even displays an easily recognizable Mount Baker, with volcanic steam decorating its cone. Few of the names recorded on this chart survived. Nevertheless, one interesting practice is revealed by this and subsequent Spanish chartings of the Northwest. Openings between landmasses—when first seen—could later turn out to be anything: rivers, bays, channels, vast canals. The Spanish tended to call them all *bocas* or mouths, until they knew more exactly what lay beyond them; so Deception Pass was Boca de Flon, and Rosario Strait was Boca de Fidalgo. Juan Francisco Eliza, who followed Quimper next year, sensed that the Ensenada de Caamano penetrated the land deeper than a bay would have and renamed it Boca de Caamano on his chart. But he decided against wasting valuable time on a canal the Indians described as tending southeastward and being too shallow for anything deeper than a canoe. What chagrin he would feel today, watching ocean liners plow steadily up those "shallows" to Seattle!

A cruise in Quimper's wake will not take long. Even if you cross the strait as he did, a few days will bring you to the end of his reconnaissance. But if you elect to follow Eliza and his men as they charted their way along new shores throughout the summer of 1791, prepare yourself for a long cruise. Thanks to the many small grocery stores in port towns and marinas, you will not have to provision your vessel for the entire excursion, but neither will you meet—as Eliza did—the friendly Clallum and Lummi Indians in laden canoes, ready to exchange fresh fish, newly dressed venison, and fruit for sheets of the "the king's copper" (used both for trading and marine repairs) and strings of beads.

Eliza's expedition consisted of two armed vessels, each equipped with a number of small tenders. Eliza himself commanded the *San Carlos,* a seventy-one-foot snow, which was the largest class of two-masted ship in use at that time. She was rigged like a brig, with square sails on both masts, but had a small trysail mast stepped just abaft the mainmast.

The second ship, commanded by José Maria Narvaez, was the *Santa Saturnina,* a thirty-five-foot schooner, less than half the length of the flagship. Two pilots made substantial contributions to the final chart, or "Carta que Comprehende," which resulted from this summer's explorations: Juan Pantoja y Arriaga, of the *San Carlos,* and Juan Carrasco, back again in familiar waters as pilot of the *Saturnina.*

Like the *Princesa Real,* the snow served as a floating headquarters for the expedition. Eliza first anchored her in Esquimalt Harbour for seventeen days. Then he crossed to Discovery Bay for a three-week anchorage; early in August he returned out the Strait of Juan de Fuca to Nootka Sound. The smaller vessel and the longboats explored Haro Strait and the western shores of the Gulf of Georgia during the time the snow lay in Esquimalt. They ran up Rosario Strait and along the British Columbia mainland coast while Eliza's ship lay in Discovery Bay. So your following cruise can actually be two separate excursions if you want it to be. The Spaniards' reports and chartings will enliven your passages as you try again to see with their eyes. Where the

Galiano Galleries (also known as Malaspina Galleries) on Gabriola Island

chartings seem incomplete, you must imagine the explorers making observations during days of fog and rain.

Pantoja and second pilot José Verdía, setting out from Esquimalt to explore the many bumps and ridges of the San Juan Islands, began by crossing Haro Strait for a look at Middle Channel. As you coast along the southwestern face of San Juan Island, you will see little that might have urged them to make more extensive explorations. Unbroken by bays or rivers, it is barren, virtually treeless, and clearly lacking water and game. Perhaps Pantoja had a bright day and could see the great cone of Mount Baker rising in the distance above this intimidating shore, as Quimper must have done and as we ourselves saw it not long ago from this same spot.

Finding that Middle Channel was only a small opening fringed by reefs and rocks (off Cattle Point) and that beyond lay a promontory stretching south again into the Strait of Juan de Fuca, Pantoja's party turned back. You may find it hard to believe the often repeated assertion that Spain's explorers thought the larger San Juan Islands together formed one solid landmass. It is more likely that, with the vastness of Haro and Rosario straits beckoning, they did not wish to spend time exploring small passages that could not lead very far in any direction.

After turning from Middle Channel—which they named Boca de Orcasitas in honor of the viceroy of New Spain—the schooner and longboat ran up Haro Strait. The commanders dotted their charts with islands where Sidney, Forrest, Domville, Coal, and the rest lie close against Vancouver Island's lee shore. They probed briefly into

Satellite Channel, noting *bocas* opening both north and south. They anchored in Fulford Harbour, and that evening Pantoja himself ran up Swanson Channel in a small tender, far enough for a glimpse of Prevost Island and still more narrow channels beyond. But the broad water of Haro Strait angling off northeastward looked more promising, so the *Santa Saturnina* set out before dawn to cross from Salt Spring to the Penders and to a first view of Bedwell Harbour. Pantoja fought head winds, which you, too, may encounter at this time of year. Anchoring here in Bedwell, and then off Patos Island, he came close to the point where he might have looked south down Rosario Strait. But he was already long overdue; so he turned back to give his report to Eliza.

You will see that Pantoja went easily halfway around the San Juans. He had seen the great canal to the north, which seemed, at last, to encourage hope of finding the Northwest Passage.

He had also charted one side of Stuart Island. He had noted and named not only Patos, but also Sucia and Matia islands. And he had looked along the high-backed ridges of Saturna, Mayne, Galiano, Valdes, and Gabriola islands and given East Point—the rocky headland that today supports a picturesque lighthouse installation—the name of Punta Santa Saturnina, in honor of his schooner. But if he suspected the presence of Trincomali Channel, he did not feel sure enough to record his suspicions.

Upon return of the two exploring vessels, Eliza's expedition sailed across Juan de Fuca to Discovery. Narvaez then set out with Carrasco to link up their summer's findings with those of Quimper at the east end of the Strait of Juan de Fuca. They concentrated this time on Rosario Strait and the Strait of Georgia, lacing up and down the intricate connecting channels for three solid weeks in July. Without stopping to look inside Deception Pass, on their charts they carefully drew in the *bocas* that separated the San Juan Islands shores: Thatcher Pass and Obstruction Pass. They charted the islands of Cypress and Guemes, poked gingerly through the shallows of Padilla, Samish, and Bellingham bays, sailed up Hale Passage, and went northwestward along the mainland as far as Texada Island, crossing the Strait of Georgia at least once, although it is difficult to say exactly where. It is interesting that, on their completed chart, Porlier Pass and Nanaimo Harbour both appear as *bocas*.

Eliza's "Carta que Comprehende" is a chart you could easily follow today, with minor adjustments. If you are lucky, you will sample some of the same extraordinary sights that impressed the Spaniards: huge pods of whales in the Strait of Georgia, a freshwater effluent (which you will recognize as the outflow of the Fraser River), a rumbling and fiery eruption indicating volcanic action in Mount Baker—

let us hope you do not see that!—and, perhaps, the beautiful, storm-carved galleries of Gabriola Island. It was the report of many whales that convinced Eliza there had to be another opening into the Strait of Georgia since, in two months on the Strait of Juan de Fuca, he himself had seen only three or four whales altogether.

Like the Spanish explorers, however, you will find no navigable access to the interior, not even far up the lower reaches of the Fraser River. The Northwest Passage was never found through Juan de Fuca.

In 1792 four more European vessels, two Spanish and two English, came through these channels and straits, to be followed by many more in subsequent years. But the 1792 explorations of Vancouver and Valdes and Galiano are too extensive for a short pleasure-craft cruise. It is enough to trace the routes of 1790 and 1791, inexact as our knowledge of them is. Surely a sense of being alone—and alien—in this extraordinary maze of islands must have struck men like Pantoja and Narvaez. With only a little effort, you can project yourself into that time and that mood.

How the Islands Got There: A Geologic Overview

The frequent bays and beaches, the dramatic, steep-sided mountain peaks, and the beautiful fjordlike water passages of the San Juan and Gulf islands are the result of a geologic history that is long, fascinating, complex, and puzzlesome. It is obvious that the San Juan Islands, in the main, represent the high points of an ancient mountain range, now partially submerged, and that the Gulf Islands are composed of long, narrow ridges running parallel to Vancouver Island to the west. Less obvious is the fact that before the mountains and ridges were formed, a series of dramatic events, spaced over eons, occurred in this region. For long ages the whole area was a tranquil sea floor, but from time to time the quiet marine scene was disturbed by episodes of earth movement, uplifting, folding of the surface, and volcanic activity.

During Permian times, 250 million years ago, volcanic eruption was especially frequent, with submarine volcanoes emerging in some places to boil the seawater as they spewed out huge flows of molten lava and hot gases. These submarine eruptions deposited the curious pillow-shaped rocks seen on Lopez Island and in a few other places in the San Juans. The times of volcanic flows were interspersed with times of relative stability, when life flourished in shallow seas, in ponds, and perhaps on reefs surrounding volcanic islands. When Permian times ended, much of the area covered today by islands and water probably stood above the level of the sea. As yet, though, the landforms bore little resemblance to the San Juan and Gulf islands we now know.

The Mesozoic era, which began 225 million years ago and lasted for 160 million years, was a time of even greater activity, featuring a sequence of profound changes in the land, which geologists have not yet fully charted. Volcanic activity continued through much of the long period, immense pressures caused the older rocks to bend and shatter, and sediments of many kinds were deposited in a fairly shallow sea. Most of Shaw Island, the central part of San Juan, and the eastern part of Orcas are covered with these rocks from the early Mesozoic. And many of the beautiful bluffs and photogenic, rounded hills are composed of rocks that date from this period.

The Cretaceous period of the later Mesozoic, between 65 and 135 million years ago, appears to have provided, for a time, a particularly hospitable environment for living things. Lush growth occurred throughout the region, to form the basis of the coal deposits widely scattered through the islands and Vancouver Island today. The Cretaceous formations at Fossil Bay on Sucia Island—a favorite place for geologists, boatmen, and souvenir hunters alike—have revealed at least ninety different species of life. Beds of the same age on Spieden, Waldron, and Skipjack have added even more to the total. This late period of the Mesozoic witnessed considerable erosion of the older surface rocks as the land rose from time to time. And, alternately, it saw the laying down of new deposits as the surface submerged. At one stage, at least, some of the island area was still clearly a part of the mainland, receiving large quantities of river sand and gravel and stream-transported soil.

Spieden, Waldron, Stuart, the Sucias, Matia, Clark, Barnes, Patos, part of Lummi, and a considerable part of the Gulf Islands are made up of rocks laid down in the Cretaceous period. Most spectacular of these rocks is the honeycombed sandstone of the Gabriola and Chuckanut formations of the very late Cretaceous, found widely along the Gulf Islands shores and in the Sucias. The strata of this period, like their predecessors, have been tilted, folded, and uplifted several times in the ages since their deposit. The constant folding was responsible for producing the landforms that in time became some of the most beautiful harbors in the islands: Long Harbour on Salt Spring, the several bays of Prevost, Reid Harbor on Stuart, and Fossil and Echo bays on Sucia. The noticeable, unidirectional (northwest-southeast) orientation of the whole Gulf Islands group reflects this ancient warping and folding.

The most impressive event of the mid-Cretaceous period in this area was the arrival of the landmass that became Vancouver Island. This landmass probably once lay to the south and west, alongside the Washington coastline, but the action of the earth's tectonic plates carried it very slowly to its current place of repose. Vancouver Island is not the only island that may have migrated. As geologists examine the strata of the San Juans and the Gulf Islands they find more and more evidence that islands that are near neighbors today originated far apart from each other, in dissimilar environments, and may have been moved close together by the earth's forces. At Blakely Island, for example, the 150-million-year-old Jurassic rocks that make up most of the island appear to have been laid down in a deep ocean, an environment not shared, so far as is known, by any of Blakely's neighbor islands.

The Cenozoic era, which lasted from the close of Mesozoic times (sixty-five million years ago) down through the great Ice Age and into the historic period, saw further dramatic changes and the slow emergence of the island landforms as we know them today. At the beginning of that era, the climate was so mild that palm trees and other warm-weather plants flourished. Their fossil remains are still easily found today. Slowly, gradually, the Strait of Juan de Fuca began to assume its outline; to the north the formation of the Strait of Georgia was taking place. Once again there was extensive folding and shattering of the older rocks, which were eroded away to be deposited as new sediments on the sea floor, where they were joined by sand and soil washed down by rivers from the mainland. By the Pliocene epoch, three million or more years ago, the Cascade and Olympic mountains had risen, with a westward extension of the Cascades reaching out into the area of the present San Juans, stretching toward Vancouver Island. Today's San Juan Islands, for the most part, represent the half-drowned remnants of that mountain extension, whose sunken valleys and ravines form the water passages and the fjordlike indentations of the shorelines. The peaks form the islands themselves.

Pleistocene times saw the coming of the massive ice sheets that pushed southward and westward from the Alaska and British Columbia mainland, covering the island area at least four times before finally retreating. In every sense, the Ice Age was the final, great sculptor that gave the islands their present appearance. Those great bodies of moving ice scraped and cut off enormous quantities of rock, scooped out the deposits of softer layers, reduced all to boulder, pebble, and sand-grain sizes, and pushed it along, together with the surface soil, eventually depositing it. Through such action, high places were ground down, rounded off, scoured, and polished, leaving ancient, long-covered rock exposed at the surface while younger rock was sometimes stripped completely away. Low spots were filled in with masses of transported rock and soil. And wherever the glaciers' forward progress stopped, and retreat started, a load of rock debris was dropped. No part of the islands was untouched by the great ice cover. Mount Constitution on Orcas Island and Mount Tuam on Salt Spring both bear the marks of glaciation.

When the ice finally retreated for the last time, some ten thousand or more years ago, evidence of its visit was everywhere in the islands. In a few cases, such as Sidney Island and its near neighbor James in the Gulf group, new islands were actually created where the huge accumulations of glacial drift were left behind. In some places, deep grooves remained in the rocks as permanent glacial scars. On a low ridge just east of Iceberg Point on Lopez and at Cattle Point on San Juan, there are striking examples of this grooving. In the old, hard rocks on southern Salt Spring, at many points on Blakely, Cypress, and Orcas, and in numerous other scattered locations where ancient igneous rocks appear at the surface, long striations bear testimony to the movement of Pleistocene ice.

Less dramatic, but perhaps the most significant legacy of the Ice Age, was the filling of low-lying areas with thick layers of glacial sand, gravel, and soil. Such deposits gave Lopez Island its present shape, joining the formerly separate island rocks of Humphrey and Upright heads with the lower elevations just to the south. Similarly, Orcas became a single island when a bridge of glacial soil closed the northern end of East Sound. Decatur, Shaw, Sinclair, and Waldron are all largely covered by glacially transported soil; most of the small, picturesque valleys on Orcas and San Juan are the same.

One additional effect of the Ice Age was the seemingly random distribution of huge boulders called erratics, some of which were transported by the ice for many miles before being dropped into their present locations. The shoreline of Lopez Island near Watmough Bay features an abundance of these erratics, as do the shores of Decatur and Cypress and, in the Gulf group, the foreshores of Sidney and James.

In the ten thousand years since the retreat of the glaciers, further changes have occurred and are still underway. First of all, there has been a broad, general uplift of the land, amounting to only a few feet in some locations and over two hundred feet in others. More obvious is the building of cliffs, beaches, and sandspits and sandbars. As the waves and currents wash into deposits of glacial gravels, sands, and soft soils along the shorelines, sea cliffs are created by the water's cutting action, and beaches are built in front of the cliffs. In addition, pebbles and tiny sand grains are carried along by currents running parallel to the shore and are finally deposited at the end of an island, laying the foundation of a spit. The spit builds slowly but steadily outward in the direction of the prevailing current, sometimes bent by the flow of water into a graceful curve. Occasionally, a spit will completely bridge a water space between an island and an offshore rock or reef, thus attaching the latter to the island. Spencer Spit on Lopez Island is an example of this process at work. Photographs taken of the spit early in the century show that a much wider water passage existed between the end of Spencer Spit and little Frost Island to the east than exists today. In time, the spit will block the passage completely and Frost Island will be annexed to Lopez.

Sidney Spit on Sidney Island is changing also, but in quite a different way. Here, a combination of winds, waves, tides, and currents is slowly eroding away the spit. In hopes of stabilizing this beautiful landform, the British Columbia Parks Branch has constructed a system of piles and logs along the area. As a result, just south of the spit, along the western edge of the marine park, the sheltered anchorage area by the old government wharf is filling in with transported sand so fast that much of it is no longer usable by boaters.

Until the next great geologic episode further alters the islands in some major way, we can anticipate that the shorelines will continue to change in small but perceptible ways. Some bays will be filled in or be closed off by bars and spits, ending up first as lagoons and then as dry sand flats; others will change appearance as beaches are moved by the waters and cliffs are cut farther back by wave and current action. Spits will grow, shrink, and sometimes alter direction as winds, currents, and tidal action dictate. And the whole island system will gradually be modified by the gentle erosion of rain, wind, winter frost, and occasional storms.

Meanwhile, the island rocks have proved economically useful as well as scenic. In the early years of this century, blacksmiths throughout the island system dug their own coal from small, exposed local seams. For many years, the limestone quarries at Roche Harbor on San Juan Island constituted the biggest industry in the region. The Sucia Islands provided sandstone paving blocks for the early streets of Seattle. Waldron Island supplied considerable rock for the building of jetties at the mouth of the Columbia River. Lopez Island has furnished building stone for contractors throughout the Northwest. The feldspar outcroppings at Deer Harbor on Orcas were worked briefly when they were found suitable for the making of porcelain. Chromite has been mined on Cypress Island. And Saturna Island still provides British Columbia with rock used in making paving material.

Crossing the Line: Customs, Fishing Licenses, and Radios

Crossing an international border is always a matter of law and of courtesy. Experienced travelers know that if they are scrupulous in observing the former and thoughtful about displaying the latter they will enjoy smooth sailing in alien waters.

The open border between Canada and the United States sometimes leads us to forget that United States citizens are aliens in Canada and that Canadian citizens are aliens in the United States. A common language, a common cultural ancestry, contiguous shorelines, and shared tidal currents all lull boatmen into thinking that no real "line" exists. But it does, and below are the rules, regulations, and courtesies you should keep in mind when venturing to cross it.

Customs

U.S. Citizens Entering Canada by Boat

You must enter Canada through a designated gateway, a customs clearing station. You may not land elsewhere in Canada until you have passed through customs. Let us look first at the locations of the various clearing stations that you might use in boating between the San Juan and Gulf islands. When headed north in a small pleasure craft you will probably consider Bedwell Harbour first. This station is a convenience established especially for you. All the *Border Boating* cruises that cross into Canada go by way of Bedwell, which serves only waterborne pleasure craft and small seaplanes. The inspectors at Bedwell are specialists in the kind of travel you enjoy. They do not waste time or effort inquiring about matters that are irrelevant to small craft. The harbor (located on the southern tip of South Pender Island) lies directly on your route north if you have just come from a cruise among the San Juan Islands or the inlets of Puget Sound, and you can enter it after using the shortest and most direct crossing of Haro Strait, between the Canadian Penders and American Stuart Island. It is a very convenient stop in summer.

But for the glorious cruising days of autumn, Bedwell Harbour will not do. It is a "seasonal office" because it opens early in May, usually on a weekend, and closes for the winter. For about the first three weeks, its hours of service (seven days a week) are from nine in the morning to five in the evening. Beginning near the end of May and lasting to early September, the hours are eight in the morning to ten in the evening, but for the rest of September they go back to the nine-to-five schedule. And on 30 September, at five in the evening, the office closes, not to reopen until May of the following year.

Anticipating an October or November crossing into Canada, you will have to decide which of the year-round customs stations is best for you. If your cruise plan lies closer to the southern part of Vancouver Island than to the northern Gulf Islands, Victoria and Sidney are your best choices. Victoria has much appeal, but if you are anxious to reach the majestic wilderness of the British Columbia coast, Sidney is a time-saving stop part way up the east side of Vancouver Island, almost on a line with Roche Harbor.

Daily hours of service for the clearance of yachts at Victoria and Sidney are eight in the morning to midnight. If you put in at Oak Bay Marina or at a yacht club's moorings near Victoria, a telephone call will summon an inspector. There is no charge for this service during regular hours, and ordinarily you do not have to wait very long, either.

It is unlikely that you will need another Canadian customs station for any of the *Border Boating* cruises. If you want to know hours and locations of small-craft customs stations on the mainland at the border (White Rock), at Vancouver, or even farther north, call (604) 666-1272, or write the Customs House, 1001 West Pender Street, Vancouver, British Columbia, V6E 2M8, Canada.

When do you report? Immediately, whatever the hour—as soon as your boat first enters a Canadian port. This is the law. If you do not report immediately, your vessel can be seized. According to the customs superintendent at Victoria, *more misunderstandings stem from failure to comply with this regulation than from any other cause.*

How do you report? By answering a few specific questions. Once an inspector appears on the wharf beside your boat, the formalities are brief and are conducted in an atmosphere of cordiality and good cheer. You will be asked where you were born and how long you plan to stay in Canada. Papers in your possession should include the boat's license, ship's registry, or papers of documentation. Every person aboard should be able to produce personal identification indicating citizenship, in case it is called for. For U.S. citizens, a driver's license will do the trick.

Note this one special regulation regarding passengers who are citizens of another country but are crossing from the United States into Canada: "Persons temporarily in the U.S., who would require visas if coming to Canada directly from their countries of origin, must now obtain Canadian non-immigrant visas if they plan to enter Canada from the U.S."

What about pets? You must have documentary proof (a veterinary's certificate) that your dog or cat has had a rabies inoculation within the previous year. Since collars can be shifted from one animal to another, a collar and rabies tag are not adequate proof of inoculation. The veterinary's certificate should contain a good description of your animal.

You will be asked about cargo. All automatic weapons are prohibited. A rifle or shotgun may be taken into Canada, provided the shotgun has a barrel that is at least twenty-six inches long. Personal prescription drugs are allowed, but nonprescription narcotics are prohibited. You are allowed enough duty-free food per person for two days, but this regulation is usually interpreted with latitude. You may take into Canada (duty free) up to 200 cigarettes and forty imperial ounces of liquor or wine (or two dozen cans of beer) per adult, nineteen years of age or older. Fresh fruits containing pits are likely to be impounded; better eat them before leaving the United States.

If your papers, passengers, and cargo are all in order, the inspector will issue you a "combined inward/outward report," which is a cruising permit. This is a small green slip of paper, which you should keep handy while in Canadian waters. No further reporting to customs is necessary once you have it. When you leave the country, your only obligation is to report to the nearest U.S. customs and immigration dock for reentry into the United States. The U.S. customs officer will probably ask for your Canadian permit, so do not throw it away.

On returning to U.S. waters from a cruise in the Gulf Islands, you will probably clear U.S. customs at the primary San Juan Island station at Friday Harbor or the seasonal station at Roche Harbor, which is also on San Juan. The customs floats in these harbors are located close to the moorage floats for small craft, and large signs guide you in. At present, hours of service at these two stations are the same as at any other vessel port of entry in the United States: eight in the morning to five in the afternoon, Monday through Saturday. These hours are in effect all year around at Friday Harbor. At Roche Harbor an inspector may not be on the floats much before Memorial Day or after Labor Day, so you are urged to go directly to Friday Harbor for clearance at other times of the year. If for some reason you must clear through Roche Harbor during other than summer seasons, be sure to do so before four in the afternoon, allowing the extra hour for the inspector to drive there from Friday Harbor. In this case, the skipper should go ashore and telephone the Friday Harbor station (378-2080) to report his arrival.

The after-hours charge for inspection of pleasure craft is

twenty-five dollars. However, because boating in the islands is subject to delays of one sort or another, the Friday Harbor Chamber of Commerce underwrites the after-hours charges between five and seven in the evening Monday through Saturday, and from nine in the morning until seven in the evening on Sundays. If you come in during those hours, the charge is only four dollars per boat. This welcome aid is supplied during the summer season, from Memorial Day to Labor Day.

Efforts are being made to extend the regular hours of service at the customs docks because of the peculiar needs of pleasure boatmen in the islands, so you might call ahead to the Friday Harbor Customs (378-2080) to determine exact hours on the day you plan to return.

Clearance on your return to U.S. waters is likely to be both simple and quick. If the moorage space at the customs float is all occupied, you idle nearby until there is room to approach, and again no one but the skipper goes ashore until you are cleared.

You may bring back to the United States thirty-two ounces of tax-free liquor per adult (twenty-one years old), if you have been out of the country for at least forty-eight hours. You may bring back 100 cigars and two cartons of cigarettes, provided that none of them comes from Cuba. Normal amounts of prescription drugs are allowed.

You must declare all purchases made in Canada. (We keep a running list, with the prices we paid and sales slips where possible, so we can hand them to the inspector on the dock. It saves time.) If you have been out of the country for less than forty-eight hours, each person aboard may bring in $10 worth of goods, tax free. If you have been gone for more than forty-eight hours, each person may bring in as much as $100 worth of goods duty free, although in this kind of boating it is unlikely that you will want to. The tax exemptions are valid once every thirty days, so if you cross the line twice in a given month you will have to pay import taxes the second time.

Fresh fruit and potatoes are often confiscated (the rule is that no citrus or potatoes may be imported unless they were grown in the United States, but the place of origin is often hard to pinpoint); meats (up to fifty pounds) and vegetables of either Canadian or U.S. origin are allowed through. Fish you catch will cause no problem so long as you conform to both Canadian and Washington State limits and licensing. Again, to avoid confusion, we usually consume most of the fresh commodities in our galley before crossing the line in either direction.

The customs inspector will ask questions concerning the above and will usually board your vessel for a quick look around. Passengers should be prepared to confirm their citizenship; boat licensing and ownership papers should be at hand.

Remember: You go immediately to a customs station as soon as you cross the line, making no other stops until you have clearance. Customs stations at port cities on the mainland (for example, Anacortes, Bellingham, Everett) may, on occasion, be your first stop, in which case the skipper must go immediately to a telephone and call the customs office to report his boat's arrival. No one else goes ashore, and the skipper must return aboard immediately after making the call and remain there until an inspector arrives.

Canadian Citizens Entering the United States by Boat

The above regulations also apply to Canadian boatmen who may be planning to follow these *Border Boating* cruises from a home port in Victoria, Nanaimo, Vancouver, or another Canadian base. They should enter the United States at Friday Harbor or at Roche Harbor during the hours described above.

The Canadian skipper will be issued a cruising permit at the U.S. customs station. It will specify the length of time he proposes to remain in the United States (up to six months maximum).

Dogs must have rabies certificates and cats must be in good health, preferably with a veterinary's certificate to that effect. However, since a recent Canadian regulation requires rabies certificates for cats being brought into Canada, the Canadian skipper must remember to start out with rabies certificates for both cat and dog.

When returning to Canadian waters, the Canadian boatman who has been cruising in U.S. waters for forty-eight hours or more may bring home, duty free, up to $50 worth of goods per person (four times a year, or once quarterly); if he has been out seven days or more, he may bring into Canada $150 worth of duty-free goods per person (one time in a year). All other regulations governing food supplies, tobacco, alcohol, prescription drugs, and firearms are the same as described above for entry into Canada or the United States.

For more information about U.S. customs, write to District Director of Customs, Room 2039, Federal Office Building, Seattle, Washington 98174, U.S.A. A useful pamphlet entitled "Know Before You Go" summarizes customs requirements for returning U.S. residents. It is for sale by the Superintendent of Documents, U.S. Government Printing Office, Washington, D.C. 20402, at fifty-five cents a copy.

For more information about Canadian customs, write to Revenue Canada, Customs and Excise, Information Unit, 1001 West Pender Street, Vancouver, British Columbia, V6E 2M8, Canada.

Fishing Licenses

Regulations governing fishing from aboard a pleasure craft in Washington State or British Columbia waters are so subject to change in these days of dispute over commercial fishing rights that we hesitate to include specific details in this book. The right of a visiting noncitizen to fish, the kind of license required and the cost thereof, the open seasons, and the catch limits may all change in a matter of months.

Therefore, if you wish to fish while cruising, be sure you secure current information, in advance, about fishing in Canadian waters by writing to License Section, Regional Headquarters, Fisheries Service, Department of the Environment, 1090 West Pender Street, Vancouver, British Columbia, V6E 2P1, Canada. For information about fishing in Washington waters, write to Washington State Department of Fisheries, 115 General Administration Building, Olympia, Washington 98504, U.S.A.

"Fishing," by the way, means the search for any kind of seafood, including clams and oysters. Always be on the lookout for signs that prohibit fishing in certain waters. They are often posted on docks where pleasure craft moor.

Radios

At present, single-side-band or VHF radios may be used without additional licensing in Canada or the United States, provided they are properly licensed in your country of residence. However, if you intend to use a CB radio on your boat, a permit for its use in the country you are visiting is required. To obtain one, write to the Regional Director, Telecommunications Regulations Branch, Department of Communications, Room 320, 325 Granville Street, Vancouver, British Columbia, V6C 1S5, Canada, or to Seattle District Office, Federal Communications Commission, 3256 Federal Building, 915 2nd Avenue, Seattle, Washington 98174, U.S.A.

Once in another country's waters, it is a courtesy for skippers to monitor local CB usage long enough to locate someone whom they can call and then to ask what channel is appropriate for use in that area, what channels are reserved for emergency calls, and so forth.

The courtesies of boating are important, as we all know, both for good will and for safety. And if you do not understand local regulations, it is always a good idea to ask someone. The Canadian Government Office of Tourism puts out a pamphlet entitled "Travel Information, Canada." Office of Tourism bureaus in western cities of the United States are located in Seattle, San Francisco, and Los Angeles. You are encouraged to address particular queries to them.

Safety Reminders

U.S. Coast Guard Requirements for Boats on American Waters
1. Fire extinguishers on all boats with enclosed spaces, the number depending on size of boat. (Even an open, outboard motorboat should carry one.)
2. A backfire flame arrester on each carburetor of a powerboat.
3. Personal flotation devices (for example, life jackets, survival suits), one approved type for each person aboard, plus one throwable device (flotation cushion or ring buoy).
4. Bell on all boats twenty-six feet or over; horn or whistle on all boats.
5. Regulation lights for night cruising and for anchoring.

It is wise to keep a copy of the U.S. *Federal Requirements for Recreational Boats* (Coast Guard Publication 290) with your charts and other printed aids. It is available at any Coast Guard station or by writing Commander, Thirteenth Coast Guard District, 618 Second Avenue, Seattle, Washington 98104.

Canadian Department of Transport Requirements for Small Vessels on Canadian Waters
1. All of the above U.S. Coast Guard requirements.
2. Two oars or paddles on all vessels under twenty-six feet.
3. Manual bailing devices (one for vessels under twenty-six feet, two for vessels twenty-six to forty feet).
4. Anchor and fifty feet of anchor line or chain for all vessels over eighteen feet.
5. Life buoy and buoyant heaving line for all vessels over twenty-six feet.
6. Distress flares for all boats over twenty-six feet.
7. Two fire buckets; also efficient bilge pump system on all vessels over forty feet.
8. A radar reflector, unless this device is impracticable.

Boats in Canadian waters should have on board the Canadian *Boating Safety Guide,* obtainable from the Coast Guard Rescue Office, Kitsilano Coast Guard Base, 1661 Whyte Avenue, Vancouver, British Columbia, V6J 1A9, Canada.

Additional Safety Items

1. Several flashlights (check batteries) and battery-powered lantern.
2. Signal flares and mirror. (On boats over twenty-six feet on Canadian waters, these are *required.*)
3. Hand axe.
4. First-aid kit.
5. Hand bilge pump or bailing scoop, in addition to the boat's built-in pump. (These are *required* on Canadian waters.)
6. Hand-operated whistle or horn, in addition to the boat's built-in horn.
7. Boat hook.
8. Extra line (one hundred feet is what we carry).
9. Dinghy for nonbeachable boat.
10. Anchor. (*Required* on Canadian waters for boats over eighteen feet.)

Float Plan

Before setting out on a cruise, leave the following information with a relative, friend, or neighbor: your itinerary, the date you expect to return, the name and radio call number of your boat, the number of passengers, and a brief physical description of your boat. When you return, be sure to notify this person; otherwise, he or she may have all the rescue forces in the area looking for you.

Radio Safety Provisions

Channel 16 on VHF radio is monitored by the U.S. Coast Guard and the Canadian Coast Guard twenty-four hours a day. In addition, both services monitor Channel 9 on CB radio when they have the man power to do so. Therefore, CB is less reliable for direct contact. However, the voluntary REACT (Radio Emergency Associated Citizens Teams) program monitors CB Channel 9. A growing number of REACT units cover the San Juan and Gulf islands area, including those of Whatcom and Skagit counties, San Juan, Camano, Victoria, Sidney, and Nanaimo.

International Distress Call Formula for Reporting an Emergency on Board Your Vessel

1. "Mayday! Mayday! Mayday! This is (give your vessel's radio call number and the vessel's name)." *Repeat this message three times.*
2. Tell where you are. Give latitude and longitude if you know them, but if not, give as accurate a statement as you can with reference to locations marked on your charts.

3. Tell what is wrong and what kind of help you need.
4. Give the number of persons aboard and the condition of any-one injured.
5. Tell how seaworthy your boat is.
6. Give a description of your boat: length, type (power or sail and general characteristics such as cabin cruiser, sloop, day boat), color of your hull, and superstructure. Rescuers will be trying to sight you through binoculars, at a distance.

Visual Distress Signals

If you have no radio aboard or if your set is not working, you should be prepared to hail a passing vessel or a person ashore by using the mariner's visual distress signals.

During daylight hours:

1. Raise and lower your outstretched arms, waving a brightly colored cloth in one or each hand. Stand on a high point on your vessel to make this signal.
2. Wave the international distress flag (fluorescent red orange) or an orange personal flotation device back and forth over your head. Canadian boatmen may have aboard the Canadian surface-to-air signal, a fluorescent orange cloth with a black circle and a black square; this signal should be used if available.
3. In U.S. waters, fly the American flag upside down.
4. Use a mirror to attract attention. Flash it at other vessels or at observers ashore.
5. Use a smoke flare, often supplied with flare kits for mariners. If no smoke flare is available, you might want to start a smoke signal by burning oily rags in a safe metal container on deck (use extreme caution).
6. Use your horn, either signaling SOS (three short blasts, three long blasts, three short blasts) or giving a long, continuous blast.

During hours of darkness:

1. Use distress flares, which should be aboard every vessel.
2. Use a flashlight, a battery-powered lantern, or your vessel's lights, flashing SOS (three short flashes, three long flashes, three short flashes).
3. Use your horn, signaling SOS or giving a long continuous blast.

Divers, Deadheads, and Drift

Diving is a popular sport in the islands, so you should look out for divers when cruising. A red flag with a white diagonal slash will be shown on a boat, rock, reef, or buoy in their vicinity.

Deadheads and drift are also common in Northwest waters. Powerboats moving at over seven knots should keep a deadhead watch for daylight cruising. At night, cruise slowly, preferably with a spotlight illuminating the water just ahead.

Helpful Charts, Addresses, and Reading

Navigation Charts

NOAA Folio Small-Craft Charts
    18423 Bellingham to Everett, including San Juan Islands
    18445 Puget Sound—Possession Sound to Olympia
Canadian Hydrographic Service Small-Craft Chart
    3310 Gulf Islands, Victoria Harbour to Nanaimo Harbour

Small-craft charts are adequate, but for people who prefer large-size charts, here is a selection from among those available.

NOAA Charts
    18421 Strait of Juan de Fuca to Strait of Georgia
    18441 Admiralty Inlet and Puget Sound to Seattle
Canadian Hydrographic Service Charts
    3450 East Point to Sand Heads
    3451 Discovery Island to Saltspring Island

Marinas and Marine Services

The following list does not include all the marinas and shipyards in the border islands, just those suggested on the cruise courses outlined in this book. For more complete information, consult the selections listed at the end of this chapter. Note that many of the marinas, particularly those in the Gulf Islands, are seasonal. They are open only from late spring to early fall.

ABC Charters, Inc., Cap Sante Boat Harbor, Anacortes, WA 98221, U.S.A.; (206) 293-5800
Anglers Anchorage Marina, Marchant Road, Brentwood Bay, B.C., Canada; (604) 652-3531
Bartel's Resort, Rt. 1, Box 1040, Eastsound, WA 98245, U.S.A.; (206) 376-2242
Bedwell Harbour Resort, South Pender Island, B.C., Canada; (604) 629-3488

Blakely Marina, Blakely Island, WA 98222 U.S.A.; (206) 375-6121

Brentwood Inn, 7172 Brentwood Drive, Brentwood Bay, B.C., Canada; (604) 652-2413

Butchart Gardens, Box 4010, Postal Station A, Victoria, B.C. V8X 3X4, Canada; (604) 652-2222

Cap Sante Marine, P.O. Box 607, Anacortes, WA 98221, U.S.A.; (206) 293-3145

Deer Harbor Marina, P.O. Box 176, Deer Harbor, WA 98243, U.S.A.; (206) 376-4420

Galiano Lodge, Sturdies Bay, Galiano Island, B.C., Canada; (604) 539-2233

Genoa Bay Marina, R.R. 1, Duncan, B.C., Canada; (604) 746-7621

Haro Hotel. *See* Roche Harbor Resort

Inn of the Sea, Yellow Point Road, R.R. 1, Ladysmith, B.C., V0R 2E0, Canada; (604) 245-4257

Islander Lopez, Fisherman Bay, Lopez, WA 98261, U.S.A.; (206) 668-2233

La Conner Country Inn, La Conner, WA 98257, U.S.A.; (206) 466-3101

La Conner Marina, P.O. Box 456, La Conner, WA 98257, U.S.A.; (206) 466-3118

Lighthouse Inn, La Conner, WA 98257, U.S.A.; (206) 466-3149

Montague Harbour Marina, Ltd., R.R. 1, Galiano, B.C., V0N 1P0, Canada; (604) 539-2461 or 539-5733

Oak Bay Marina, 1327 Beach Drive, Victoria, B.C., Canada; (604) 598-3366

Olga Store, P.O. Box 86, Olga, WA 98279, U.S.A.; (206) 376-4238

Page Marina and Store, Silva Bay, Gabriola Island, B.C., Canada; (604) 247-9241

Port Browning Marina, North Pender Island, General Delivery, Port Washington, B.C., V0H 2T0, Canada; (604) 629-3493

Roche Harbor Resort, Roche Harbor, WA 98250, U.S.A.; (206) 378-2155

Rosario Resort Hotel, Eastsound, WA 98245, U.S.A.; (206) 376-2222

San Juan Marina (at Friday Harbor), P.O. Box 340, Friday Harbor, WA 98250, U.S.A.; (206) 378-2841

Silva Bay Resort Hotel, Gabriola Island, B.C., V0R 1X0, Canada; (604) 247-9267

Silva Bay Shipyard, Ltd., Gabriola Island, B.C., V0R 1X0, Canada; (604) 247-9317

Skyline Marina, Inc., Flounder Bay, Anacortes, WA 98221, U.S.A.; (206) 293-5134 (Note: Skyline Marina provides charter service.)

Snug Harbor Marina Resort (on Mitchell Bay, San Juan Island). Friday Harbor, WA 98250, U.S.A.; (206) 378-4762

Springwater Lodge, Ltd., (on Active Pass), Box 39, Mayne Island, B.C., Canada; (604) 539-5521

Telegraph Harbour Marina, Thetis Island, B.C., Canada; (604) 246-9511

Thetis Island Marina, Telegraph Harbour, Thetis Island, B.C., Canada; (604) 246-9733

Village Point Marina, 4232 Legoe Bay Drive, Lummi Island, WA 98262, U.S.A.; (206) 758-2565

West Sound Bay Marina, Inc., P.O. Box 19, Orcas, WA 98280, U.S.A.; (206) 376-2314

Parks in the San Juan Islands

For information write to District Supervisor, District III, Region II, State Parks and Recreation Commission, P.O. Box 487, Burlington, WA 98233, U.S.A.

Parks in the Gulf Islands

For information write to District Supervisor, Parks Branch, 2930 Trans-Canada Highway, Victoria, B.C. V8X 3X2, Canada.

Helpful Reading

Berssen, William. *Pacific Boating Almanac: Pacific Northwest and Alaska.* Ventura, Calif.: Western Marine Enterprises, annual.

Calhoun, Bruce. *Cruising the San Juan Islands.* Newport Beach, Calif.: Sea Publications, Inc., 1973.

Cole, Phil and Gwen, eds. "1978 Cruising Guide." *Northwest Boat Travel* (Mount Vernon, Wash.) I (1).

Easterbrook, Don J. and Rahm, David A. *Landforms of Washington: The Geologic Environment.* Bellingham, Wash.: Union Printing Company, 1970.

Evergreen Cruising Atlas: From Queen Charlotte Sound to Olympia. Seattle: Straub Printing and Publishing, 1978.

Hamilton, Bea. *Salt Spring Island.* Vancouver, B.C.: Mitchell Press, 1969.

Hilson, Stephen E. *Exploring Puget Sound and British Columbia.* Holland, Mich.: Van Winkle Publishing Co., 1975.

Richardson, David. *Pig War Islands.* Eastsound, Wash.: Orcas Publishing Co., 1971.

Scheffer, Victor B. *Messages from the Shore.* Seattle: Pacific Search Press, 1977.

Smith, Lynwood S. *Living Shores of the Pacific Northwest.* Seattle: Pacific Search Press, 1976.

Waaland, J. Robert. *Common Seaweeds of the Pacific Coast*. Seattle: Pacific Search Press, 1977.

Wahl, Terence R. and Paulson, Dennis R. *A Guide to Bird Finding in Washington*. Bellingham, Wash.: Terence Wahl, 1977.

Wolferstan, Bill. *Cruising Guide to the Gulf Islands*. Vancouver, B.C.: Pacific Yachting Interpress Publications, 1976.

Other Books from Pacific Search Press

Asparagus: The Sparrowgrass Cookbook by Autumn Stanley

Bone Appétit! Natural Foods for Pets by Frances Sheridan Goulart

Butterflies Afield in the Pacific Northwest by William Neill/Douglas Hepburn, photography

The Carrot Cookbook by Ann Saling

Cascade Companion by Susan Schwartz/Bob and Ira Spring, photography

Common Seaweeds of the Pacific Coast by J. Robert Waaland

The Crawfish Cookbook by Norma S. Upson

Cross-Country Downhill and Other Nordic Mountain Skiing Techniques by Steve Barnett

The Dogfish Cookbook by Russ Mohney

The Ferry Story by Terry Lawhead/illustrated by Paula Richards

Fire and Ice: The Cascade Volcanoes by Stephen L. Harris

The Green Tomato Cookbook by Paula Simmons

Little Mammals of the Pacific Northwest by Ellen B. Kritzman

Living Shores of the Pacific Northwest by Lynwood Smith/Bernard Nist, photography

Make It and Take It: Homemade Gear for Camp and Trail by Russ Mohney

Marine Mammals of Eastern North Pacific and Arctic Waters edited by Delphine Haley

Messages from the Shore by Victor B. Scheffer

Minnie Rose Lovgreen's Recipe for Raising Chickens by Minnie Rose Lovgreen

Rhubarb Renaissance: A Cookbook by Ann Saling

The Salmon Cookbook by Jerry Dennon

Sleek & Savage: North America's Weasel Family by Delphine Haley

Spinning and Weaving with Wool by Paula Simmons

Starchild & Holahan's Seafood Cookbook by Adam Starchild and James Holahan

Why Wild Edibles? The Joys of Finding, Fixing, and Tasting by Russ Mohney

Wild Mushroom Recipes by Puget Sound Mycological Society

Wild Shrubs: Finding and Growing Your Own by Joy Spurr

The Zucchini Cookbook by Paula Simmons